VIA MEDIA

VIA MEDIA

An Essay in
Theological Synthesis

E.L. MASCALL
Foreword by Andrew Davison

Quatuor quoque circulos aureos praeparabis.
—Exod. xxv: 26
Statuisti in loco spatioso pedes meos.
—Ps. xxx: 9

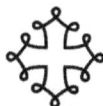

Angelico Press

Cover design
by Michael Schrauzer

REVERENDISSIMO AC HONORATISSIMO IN CHRISTO PATRI AC DOMINO

DOMINO MICHAELI

PROVIDENTIA DIVINA

ARCHIEPISCOPO EBORACENSI

ANGLIAE PRIMATI

HOC OPUSCULUM

OBSERVANTER AMANTERQUE

DEDICAVIT AUCTOR

CONTENTS

FOREWORD
TO THE ANGELICO PRESS EDITION
(2025)

BY ANDREW DAVISON

Eric Mascall's *Via Media* is one of the more remarkable
short surveys of Christian doctrine from the past century. Especially audacious is what Mascall places center
stage, and what he passes over. There are only four chapters: on Creation, the Trinity, the Incarnation, and Grace.
Soteriology, in the sense of sin and redemption, loses
out to grace and deification.

That Mascall was able to achieve what he wanted in
four chapters was clearly important to him—clearly, at
least, if we allow our eyes to linger on the title page, with
its quotation from the Book of Exodus: *Quatuor quoque
circulos aureos praeparabis* ("You shall prepare four rings
of gold"). Pleasingly ring-like, we might also note, is the
way in which the conclusion ends by looping back to
the first chapter, the relation of the creature to God, so
central to the doctrine of creation, being the basis for its
openness to grace.

If Mascall's *Via Media* is a somewhat curtailed systematics, and in that respect rather innovative, then also arrest-
ing is how conservative it was for 1956, and indeed that
he wrote it at all. Writing surveys of Christian doctrine

was generally not the way of things in the Church of England of that time, especially not with Mascall's confidence in the worth of old texts and formulations, nor (God forbid!) as a Thomist. His contemporaries turned their hand to a wide range of theological genres: historical, philosophical, homiletic, ethical, and biblical. They wrote erudite essays. They wrote about making Christian faith and life "relevant in the modern age." They did not write confident surveys of doctrine.

The nearest we get to *Via Media* among comparable figures is John Macquarrie's *Principles of Christian Theology* (1966), doing for existentialism what Mascall had for Thomism. Admittedly, from William Temple we have *Christian Faith and Life* (1931), but that is altogether more popular in tone, with a theological depth that does not compare with Mascall's.

Short Anglican systematics were more a late nineteenth-century endeavor. Examples on the Catholic side include Francis Hall's *Doctrinal Outlines* (1892, published in one volume with revisions by Frank Hudson Hallock in 1933, and still useful), Alfred Mortimer's *Catholic Faith and Practice* (1896 — like Hall, Mortimer was an American), and Darwell Stone's *Outlines of Christian Dogma* (1900). On the evangelical side, there is H. C. G. Moule's *Outlines of Christian Doctrine* (1889).

The title *Via Media* obviously trades on the idea of the Church of England and the Anglican tradition as a "middle way" between Geneva and Rome. Also in view is a middle way between moderation and comprehensiveness, although the main structuring principle of the text is the middle way between heresies. Those historical theological mistakes typically took too extreme or exclusive a position on some question. Compared to that, orthodoxy manages to avoid the extremes, while holding together the truth that opposed heresies championed in too shrill or exclusionary a fashion. Thus—to work through the chapters—in the doctrine of creation we are to uphold both the dependence of creation upon God (since creation is not self-founded) and its reality (since it is not an illusion, not to be considered unreal, as if some comparison between God and creatures were possible). In the doctrine of the Trinity we have the eternal archetype of that relation in the derived equality of the Son and the Spirit (although the procession of the Spirit is by no means a focus): that the Son is "equal to the Father, but equal with a derived equality." The same idea opens the chapter on Christology, where a middle way is also necessary between stressing his divinity and his humanity, and between stressing their union and their distinction. In the final chapter, on grace, our middle way affirms both that the creature is never other than a creature and that it can be elevated to share in the divine life, and that grace is both a gift that could not be demanded and at the same time nature's fulfillment, not its abolition, nor alien to it.

In these tensions and middle ways, I am reminded of one of the twenty-first century's most valuable single-volume works of systematic theology so far (although much longer than *Via Media*): Mauro Gagliardi's *Truth Is a Synthesis: Catholic Dogmatic Theology* (2020, published in Italian in 2017). Gagliardi has a similar interest to Mascall, in holding pairs together according

to what he calls the "and... and..." logic of Catholic theology (rather than "either... or..."). These include creation and God, nature and grace, this life and the world
to come. To this, Gagliardi adds that in each pair, one
typically grounds and enfolds the other—these are not
equal pairings, as Christ's divinity creates his humanity
and makes it personal, and as grace both precedes nature
(since nature is an undeserved gift) and perfects it. This
second stage of argument is worth adding. It would not
be contentious to Mascall, but he does not spell it out
as Gagliardi does.

Although seventy years old, Mascall's book has a
contemporary ring. Consider his open-hearted interest in other religions. His desire is always to sing the
glories of Christianity, but he is also convinced that
grace works beyond the bounds of the Church. Alongside that, we might mention his warmth towards the
ancient churches with "miaphysite" Christology. They
may stress unity of Christ's divinity and humanity in
a way that has left Chalcedonian Christianity uneasy,
but Mascall would rather stress our common faith (as,
more recently, would various important recent Christological agreements). Also rather twenty-first-century
is the lack of any sense that Christianity needs to
be revisionary in its doctrine, of crisis, of being on
the back foot, or of being positioned by modernity.
Equally notable is Mascall's awareness of the significance of Aquinas's Platonism (by no means widely
or sufficiently recognized by prominent Continental
Thomists at the time). The language of participation,
for instance, is ubiquitous. His emphasis on deification

was also a recovery ahead of its time. Finally, consider Mascall's diagnosis that the Reformation suffered from not shaking itself *sufficiently* free from the doctrinal and philosophical legacy of the late Middle Ages—of the "'most irremediably vitiated and corrupt' elements of late medieval thought" (quoting Louis Bouyer). In that sense, philosophically, the Reformation was not sufficiently "radical," as Mascall put it.

Via Media is not without weaknesses. Some readers will count its fleeting treatment of sin and salvation among them, although its elevation of grace over sin perhaps says something rather beautiful. On the scholarly front, Mascall had a tendency to work with primary texts and ideas through secondary ones, among whom George Leonard Prestige features prominently. Likewise, rather extraordinarily, the bibliography does not direct the inquisitive reader to a single text by the likes of Augustine, Aquinas, John of the Cross, or Theresa of Avila, although they all feature in the book.

For someone so animated by old texts and ideas, Mascall's investment in contemporary "secondary" discussions is a little incongruent; but it was his way. His 1963 book *Theology and Images*, for instance, devotes inordinate space to criticism of the now unknown A. C. Bridge. Another book from the same year, *Up and Down in Adria*, is devoted to what he thinks about the *Soundings* collection (edited by Alec Vidler). Perhaps, being charitable, we might take this as a sign of modesty on Mascall's part: he placed himself firmly among the figures of his day, yet they were mostly destined to be lost to history, while Mascall's star has risen.

There is perhaps also an instructive example for us here. Mascall's lasting contributions came from commending and explaining the Christian tradition, more than from rebutting others.

Via Media was published in 1956, a quarter of the way through Mascall's half century of writing. Having read it, the reader may wish to explore its themes at greater length, or from different angles, in some of Mascall's other writing. For the more metaphysical aspects of the doctrine of creation, there is his *Existence and Analogy* (1949), while *The Importance of Being Human* (1974) looks at the part of creation that most interests us: ourselves. His *Christian Theology and Natural Science* (1956) also fits here. On the doctrine of God, the obvious recommendations are *He Who Is* from the beginning of Mascall's career (1943) and *The Triune God* (1986) from towards the end. With the Incarnation, we again have an early book and a later one: *The God-Man* (1940) and *Jesus: Who He is, and How We Know Him* (1985). On nature and grace, the two short volumes are *Grace and Glory* (1961, which also supplies more by way of eschatology) and *Nature and Supernature* (1976). Other books augment the themes covered in *Via Media*, notably the Church and sacramental theology (worked out in close relation to Christ) in *Christ, the Christian and the Church* (1946) and *Corpus Christi* (1965). For a sense of Mascall's life, we have his memoirs in *Saraband* (1992). Among the small collection of secondary literature, H. P. Owen wrote an obituary in the *Proceedings of the British Academy* (vol. 84, 1994, 409–418) and Brian Hebblethwaite provided the short biography in the *Oxford Dictionary of National Biography* (2004).

Via Media is my favorite work of Mascall's, a theologian for whom I feel such ready affection. It is a joy to be able to commend it to a new readership, and to do so just as I take up a post at Christ Church in Oxford: the college where Mascall taught and the cathedral in whose grounds he is buried. Those of us teaching and writing theology in the Anglican tradition today owe much to his patient, then unfashionable labours, and I hope that members of other churches may also come to appreciate this greatest of Anglican Thomists.

The Revd Professor Andrew Davison
Regius Professor of Divinity, University of Oxford
Feast of St John the Evangelist, 2025

PREFACE

Catholicity is universality, inclusiveness, as etymology itself proclaims; so we are often told. And the glory of the Church of England is its comprehensiveness; we are often told this, too. And so the Church of England can rest secure in its catholicity, for what could be more universal and inclusive than comprehensiveness?

This, however, is only one half of the picture, for we are told also, and sometimes in the same breath, that the glory of the Church of England is its moderation, that it treads with sober cheerfulness the *via media* between the vulgar flamboyancy of Rome and the dismal severity of Geneva; and it is not at all obvious that moderation and comprehensiveness are compatible. A *via media* like other *viae*, is a narrow path separating broad tracts of varied country; comprehensiveness is not *prima facie* one of the qualities we shall expect to find in it.

Nevertheless, I am sure that Anglicans have been right in holding that Christian orthodoxy in some strange way at one and the same time holds a middle position between the various heresies and also includes whatever positive truths those heresies contain. There are, of course, various ways in which this situation might be envisaged. It might, for example, be supposed that

xix

orthodoxy was simply what statisticians would describe as the weighted mean of the heresies; that in order to find out what orthodoxy was, all you would need to do would be to add up all the heresies, giving each of them its appropriate numerical coefficient and where necessary prefixing it with a minus sign, and then dividing by the sum of the coefficients. Such a view, making the very essence of truth depend upon falsehood, could hardly be taken seriously in theory by anyone, though I think that something like it is very frequently to be found in practice. It might, on the other hand, be supposed that the heresies are simply irrelevant to orthodoxy, that they have nothing in common with it whatever; that they are, as it were, pure forms of error owing nothing to the truth. This, again, I think, seems unlikely, for it is an essential principle of Christian philosophy that evil has no positive being of its own but is necessarily a defect in something that is good. In some way or another we are, I think, bound to hold that heresies arise when one aspect or element of orthodoxy gets detached from the rest and develops on its own without the controlling and balancing influence which the others would be capable of bringing to bear on it. The detached element may become stunted or hypertrophied as circumstances may dictate, and even if by some chance it more or less retains its original shape its detachment from the other elements will inevitably lead it to exercise a one-sided and exaggerated influence upon thought and practice. Nevertheless the fact remains that whatever is positive in heresy must be something essentially orthodox; and the way in which orthodoxy treads the *via media* between the heresies is—to change the metaphor—by rectifying, appropriating and reconciling their several affirmations. And—need it be added?—by doing this, orthodoxy finds itself enriched and strengthened.

Now the position which I wish to maintain in the present book is this: that on the cardinal points of Christian doctrine orthodoxy consists in holding together two notions which might well seem to be incompatible. I do not mean that they are incompatible in fact; the idea that Christianity involves believing contradictions seems to me to be as stultifying and immoral as the view that it involves clutching at one of the horns of any ostensible dilemma. A naïve 'both-and' programme and a naïve 'either-or' programme both provide scope for theological pyrotechnics but little for steady illumination. My point is simply (1) that the two notions may very well *seem* to be incompatible; (2) that if we assume that they are *really* incompatible we shall be tempted to opt for one of them to the exclusion of the other and so to fall into error; but (3) that if we go on to enquire how they must be understood if they are *not* to be incompatible we shall acquire a very much more profound understanding of the question at issue than we had when we began. And I think that, as a matter of history, we can see that the Church herself entered on just such a process of deepening her theological understanding when the proliferation of heresies compelled her to examine more closely the faith which had been committed to her.

This, then, is the thesis which I have tried to illustrate by discussing four specific examples. The first is that of creation; the dual notion of the world as possessing a dependent reality holds a middle place between atheistic positions which affirm its reality but deny its dependence and acosmist positions which affirm its dependence but deny its reality. My second example is that of the processions in the Holy Trinity; the dual notion of derived equality holds a middle place between modalist positions which affirm the equality but deny the derivation and Arian positions which affirm the derivation but deny the equality. My third example is that of the Incarnation; the Chalcedonian doctrine of the unconfused union of the two natures in Christ holds a middle place between Nestorian positions which affirm the unconfusion but deny the union and monophysite positions which affirm the union but deny the unconfusion. My fourth example is that of the traditional Catholic doctrine of grace as conferring a condition of deified creaturehood; this holds the middle position between certain aberrations of a mystical type, which stress the deification to the destruction of the creaturehood, and the attitude of Reformation Protestantism, which stresses the creaturehood but denies the deification. All these questions are, of course, very much more complex than the summary just given would suggest, as the subsequent discussion will show. It will also appear, I hope, that by approaching our several themes from the standpoint just indicated we shall not only see that the Catholic view succeeds in being both medial and comprehensive, but also that a great deal of light is thrown upon a number of incidental matters. It is for this reason that I have not resisted the temptation to digress from the main theme of a chapter whenever some attractive avenue has shown itself at the side. My discussion makes no claim to be exhaustive; it merely represents an attempt to make four applications of a promising line of thought.

If this book should fall into the hands of any philosophers of the strict logical empiricist school I am fairly sure that they will write most of it off as nonsense, though it might perhaps provide them with some material for the study of the linguistic habits of those interesting anthropoids the theologians. What conceivable cash-value, they will ask, can attach to a phrase like 'deified creaturehood'? By what standard of verifiability can it be held that there is a real issue of fact between two people who respectively affirm and deny that in Christ there is a human hypostasis? I can only say that, while linguistic analysis can perform a valuable service for theologians by warning them of the danger of sheer verbalism—a danger of which the late Middle Ages and the Counter-Reformation can provide us with only too many instances—what makes a statement intelligible is not its conformity to some antecedently prescribed canon of meaningfulness but the fact that it can be understood. Like other types of specialized discourse, theological discourse has its own laws of behaviour and exacts its own type of training if it is to be used fruitfully. But, like most other techniques, the technique of theological discourse can only be learnt by practice. And, since theological discourse is about God and the things of God, the practice which is needed is not only practice in theological discussion but practice in the Christian religion. In the last resort it is the knowledge of God which makes the theologian, not the knowledge of theology, still less the knowledge of theological linguistics. Theological discussion is bound to involve technicalities, and its language inevitably reflects the crises and controversies through which the Church has passed in the two thousand years of its history. But what it is concerned with is the life of Christian men and women in Christ, and it is in the hope that some at least of my readers may recognize that I have written about realities with which they themselves are acquainted that I venture to offer them this book.

E. L. M.

My thanks are due to Professor R. C. Zachner for his advice on certain points in the first chapter concerning Hinduism, and to Mrs. Prestige and the Society for Promoting Christian Knowledge for permission to quote from the works of the late Dr. G. L. Prestige, whose recent death has inflicted such a loss upon patristic and theological studies.

I

DEPENDENT REALITY
THE DOCTRINE OF CREATION

I. CHRISTIAN THEISM AND THE ALTERNATIVES

To those who have grown up in a civilization which, however secularized its outlook may have become, is Christian in its intellectual ancestry, the assertion that the world is a dependent reality may perhaps seem to be lacking in likelihood or even in significance, but it is more likely to appear platitudinous than paradoxical. 'I believe in God the Father almighty, maker of heaven and earth' is the opening affirmation of the Apostles' Creed; we may think that this statement is preposterous or nonsensical, but at least the idea that the world depends for its existence upon the creative act of a self-existent and omnipotent deity is familiar and unprovocative. Whether we believe in God or not, this is what belief in God means. It comes therefore as something of a surprise when we turn either to the pre-Christian thought of Greece and Rome or to the thought of the great non-Christian religions today and see that the conjunction of the notions of reality and dependence is anything but obvious to the unaided human mind.

Furthermore, when we look into the tradition of Christianity itself, we see that even there the conjunction has sometimes been difficult to maintain, and that beneath the surface of the verbal formulae the two notions have at times tended to drift apart, as in the instance of deism to which I shall shortly refer.

What, then, is this Christian assertion that the world is a dependent reality? It is the assertion that the beings of which the world is composed, many of which are known to us through the experience of our senses, are not just phantoms, masks or pseudonymous labels, concealing the antics of a deity who, for some reason known if at all only to himself, prefers to act under a variety of incognitos rather than under his own name, but are centres of real though limited spontaneity, exercising genuine energies and causal activities, while they are nevertheless entirely dependent, for their origin, their continued existence and every aspect of their activity, upon the incessant creative and personal act of a transcendent and omnipotent God, who is totally self-existent and self-sufficient. I have discussed elsewhere some of the problems to which this assertion gives rise and some of the consequences which follow from it;[1] at the moment I am concerned chiefly to make it plain what the assertion is in fact asserting. It will, however, be as well to remind ourselves of the extent to which the assertion, when it is accepted, alters the perspective under which the great philosophical and theological questions present themselves; how, for example, it forces us to realize that

----

[1] Cf. *He Who Is*, chh. viii and x; *Existence and Analogy*, ch. vi.

the fundamental problem is not whether the existence of the world necessarily implies the existence of a Creator, but why, if there is a self-existent and self-sufficient God, he should create a world at all. What I wish to do now is to illustrate the difficulty which the human mind has experienced in holding together these two notions of reality and dependence, and how it has tended to look upon the world as either, on the one hand, real but independent or, on the other hand, as dependent but unreal. What these somewhat cryptic phrases precisely mean will, I hope, become clearer as we proceed. I ought, however, to warn the reader at the start that we shall be faced with two difficulties. The first arises from the extreme instability of both these positions and the kaleidoscopic way in which they tend to pass into each other; the second from the fact that both of them tend to appear in somewhat impure and mixed forms. And I shall want to suggest that both this instability and this impurity arise from the fact that the positions in question are in fact erroneous. With these caveats in mind, it may make for greater clarity if I set out in the following tabular form the positions which I intend to consider.

1. Views of the world as real and independent:
    (i) Atheistic, naturalistic and pluralistic.
        (*a*) Dialectical materialism.
        (*b*) Scientific humanism.
        (*c*) A mitigated form: Deism.
    (ii) Pantheistic and monistic:

      (*a*) Nature mysticism.

      (*b*) Spinoza, Hegel.

2. Views of the world as dependent and unreal:

      (i) Platonism.

      (ii) Malebranche.

      (iii) Berkeley (?).

3. A mixed type: the external world dependent and unreal, but the human soul real and independent: Hinduism, in general.

First, then, to consider those views which treat the world as real and independent. These, as I have indicated in the table, fall into two very sharply contrasted classes. The first of these I have described as atheistic, naturalistic and pluralistic; for it, the world which our senses reveal to us is the only reality that there is, and our attitude to it is that of the scientific investigator and manipulator. The dialectical materialism which is the basis of Marxist Communism is one form of this; the scientific humanism, which is the implicit assumption of most people and the explicit doctrine of some scientists in our western industrialized civilization, is another. In either form its most notable characteristic is that it is fundamentally irreligious. It does not substitute some creature for God as the object of religious worship; it simply does not worship at all. It is, of course, true that even in a secularized civilization human beings find it difficult to do without some object upon which to direct the ineradicable religious *emotional* needs of the human soul; such an object may be found in the world-proletariat, the Communist Party, the idols of the cinema-screen, the symphonies of Beethoven, or anything else. But such a cultus while it may be a substitute for religion, is not a religion in the strict sense; its object is not asserted to be the source from which the world that our senses display to us proceeds or the ground upon which it depends for its existence. The cultic object has an emotional but not a cosmological function. No reason is felt to be needed for the world's existence; the world exists in its own right, it is simply 'there'. And although it is the ultimate reality, it has no claims upon man's allegiance; it is simply material for him to exploit.

I have described Deism as a mitigated form of this view, and I must explain what I mean by this. Deism is a doctrine which was highly influential in the eighteenth century and which attempted to combine an attenuated belief in a Creator with a whole-hearted acceptance of the current mechanistic physics which derived from the tremendous synthesis of Sir Isaac Newton. It has been described as follows:

> The fabric of the universe is supposed to stand to God in the relation which the instrument bears to its maker. . . . The heavens are the work of his hands, just as the watch is the work of the watchmaker. As the craftsman determines the characteristic properties of his machine, the correlation of its parts, their positions and their functions, so is God conceived to have dealt with the world. He brought it into being and ordained its laws. He imparted to it once for all the energy which serves as the driving power of the stupendous mechanism. The Deist recognises in God the ultimate

source of matter and motion, and, consistently with this conception, admits the possibility of occasional interferences on the part of the Deity. But, though the possibility of such interference is granted, the probability is called in question. It seems more in accordance with the principles of Deism that Nature should be left to work itself out in obedience to laws, originally given. . . . A perfect machine, it is supposed, would not require from time to time to be adjusted by its maker; nor would the Unchangeable introduce any later corrections into a creation which from the first reflected his omniscience and omnipotence.[1]

It is clear that Deism represents an ingenious attempt to get the best of two worlds, the world of deterministic Newtonian physics and the world of religion. For practical purposes the world can be treated as if it was the ultimate reality and as if God did not exist; for, apart from the very unlikely event of some *ad hoc* divine intervention, no present activity of God is to be found in the world at all. On the other hand, God is to be venerated as the Great Original, who called the world into existence, endowed it with its energy, and decreed the laws according to which it was to operate; the universe manifests his wisdom and his skill in much the same way as the theory of the complex variable manifests the wisdom and skill of Cauchy, or the Ninth Symphony the wisdom and skill of Beethoven. Admittedly, God still exists and it pleases him when we address our praises to him, but so far as his doing anything is concerned that is finished and done with long ages ago. The surprising

[1] G. C. Joyce, *Encyc. of Religion and Ethics*, IV, p. 541, s.v. 'Deism'.

thing about Deism is that anyone should have been able to derive religious satisfaction from so glacial a cultus; men had no doubt to be grateful for the small mercies that contemporary science was prepared to concede to them. Any claims that Deism may have had are now defunct, since physical science itself has lost its former deterministic character. It remains, however, as an interesting specimen in the Museum of Religious Archaeology; and I think it will now be plain why I described it as a mitigated form of the view which sees the world as the ultimate reality.

The view of the world as real and independent need not, however, take an atheistic, naturalistic and pluralistic form; it may take a very different form which is pantheistic and monistic. In this the world is still taken as the ultimate reality, but, so far from God's existence being denied, he (if indeed the personal pronoun is properly applicable) is identified with the world itself. The plurality and mutability of the phenomenal realm perceived by our senses is of course recognized, but it is looked upon as deceptive and illusory. If we used the word 'world' to describe the realm of phenomena, we should have to describe this view as one which denied the existence of the world rather than as one which affirmed it. However, in such views as we are considering, the phenomenal realm, however illusory its sensible characteristics may be, is held to be, as it were, a tightly fitting garment clothing an underlying 'real world' which is not only self-sufficient but is divine. What makes this plain is the fact that the object of religious worship is

sought in the underlying substance of the world itself
and not by turning one's back upon it. This attitude is
exemplified in the various forms of nature-worship and
nature-mysticism, and in immanentist philosophies as
different from one another as are those of Spinoza and
Hegel.

Turning now to those systems which view the world
as dependent but unreal, the supreme example is provided by the Platonist tradition in all its phases. For the
Platonist, the world in which we live exists, in whatever
sense it may be said to exist, solely because it imperfectly
reflects or participates in the ideal forms, but its dependence upon the ideas does not give it a status of
reality. Reality in the proper sense belongs only to the
divine realm where 'the ideal rabbit is laid up in heaven
and sports no more in the fields'. The world of which
we are part is fundamentally *un*real; that is why the laws
of mathematics only approximately apply to it. If a
Platonist gets slightly different results every time that he
measures a material object, he will not say that this is
due to his measuring technique being inaccurate, but
that it is due to the object being unreal and imperfect.
If he finds that the angles of a material triangle do not
add up to exactly 180 degrees, he will not blame himself
for having applied to an object that was not precisely
rectilinear theorems that would apply exactly only to
rectilinear objects; he will say that the triangle was a bad
and unreal triangle. He will not try to develop a theory
which will apply more accurately than the existing one
to the kinds of objects of which the world actually con-

sists; he will turn away from the material world altogether and contemplate instead the eternal world of ideas where triangles are well conducted and the sum of their angles is precisely, and not merely approximately, equal to two right angles. Only the ideal realm is fully intelligible; of it alone can we have knowledge, *epistēmē*. The realm in which we live is only intelligible at all because it remotely resembles and incompetently copies the ideal one; we can never hope to have knowledge of it, but only that highly precarious and deceptive substitute for knowledge whose name is 'opinion' or *doxa*.

In modern philosophy perhaps the clearest example we can find of the view that the world is dependent but unreal is provided by the Occasionalism of the successors of Descartes, Geulincx and Malebranche. Malebranche's doctrine has been summarized in the following words:

> There is but *one* true cause: all the rest are occasional, therefore not in truth causal at all. God is the only cause. In comparison with him, natural things are not less causal, but not *causes at all*, not causes in the relative sense, but, in the strict understanding of the term, not causes at all. . . . Malebranche states with the utmost emphasis that the contrast between false and true, pagan and Christian, philosophy consists in the affirmation and denial of secondary causes. He insists upon their absolute denial. . . . To exert a power of causality is to create: to be a cause is to be God. . . . To admit secondary causes is to affirm paganism.[1]

When we reflect that Malebranche was a devout Ora-

[1] K. Fischer, *Descartes and his School*, p. 559.

torian priest, we can form some faint idea of the extent to which by the seventeenth century the tradition of Christian philosophy had become corrupted. To Malebranche even the doctrine of St. Thomas Aquinas appeared as a form of paganism. Not even Calvin went quite as far as this in his unbalanced emphasis upon the sovereignty of God.

In my tabular summary I have given, as a third example of the view that the world is dependent but unreal, the idealism of Berkeley; but I have felt obliged to insert a question-mark after his name, for reasons which I shall now explain. So far as his ultimate doctrine of *material* objects is concerned, Berkeley seems to me to provide as pure an example as we could find of the type of view which we are now considering. Material objects have no reality whatever in themselves, and they exercise no kind of energy or activity; they are simply ideas in the mind of God, and the activity which is discernible in them is not their activity but his. There are, however, two qualifications which we must make. In the first place, however idealistic Berkeley's conception of material objects may be, his starting-point is thoroughly realistic as regards *minds*. Secondly, his fundamental assertion about material objects is not that they are ideas in the mind of God, but that they are ideas in the mind of someone; *esse* is *percipi*, but not necessarily *percipi a Deo*. It is only when he wishes to provide for the existence of material objects at the times when no finite percipients are perceiving them that Berkeley is driven to recall that they are always being perceived by God. Once this point has been reached, however, the whole perspective changes; it is their perception by God that constitutes the existence of material objects, not their perception by us. Berkeley never goes to the point of asserting that created spirits are merely dreamed by God, in the way in which, according to Tweedledee, Alice in *Through the Looking Glass* was being dreamed by the Red King, but he does come very close to this in his view of material objects. The question-mark in our table ought perhaps to be a rather large one, but I do not think that we need remove Berkeley's name. To find an absolutely pure example of the position which we are considering would, I suppose, be impossible, unless we were to take seriously the suggestion made by one of Chekhov's characters in his moments of intoxication, that perhaps we don't really exist but only think we do. To look upon ourselves as unreal is virtually impossible, and to look upon the world around us as non-existent is almost as difficult. The nearest one can get to an absolutely acosmist doctrine is to hold that the world is a kind of cinema-show put on by God. To be an absolute acosmist is impossible, but many philosophers have tried to be as acosmist as it is possible to be.

It is, I think, worth while to remark at this point upon the ease with which the positions which I have numbered 1 (ii) and 2 can pass into each other, in spite of their theoretical opposition; this is an example of the instability which I have already mentioned. We may start off by holding that the world is really divine, but if we do so we are almost bound, unless we are prepared to

worship cats and cows and crocodiles in the crudest polytheistic way, to explain, both to ourselves and to others,
that we do not attribute this exalted divine status to the
phenomenal realm—to the visible and tangible objects
of everyday experience—but to some invisible and in-
tangible substratum, of which the phenomenal realm is
a modification, manifestation or aspect. Considered in
abstraction from this divine and not easily discernible
substratum, the phenomenal realm—the 'world' of our
everyday non-religious experience—is essentially unreal
and illusory. Thus the pantheist can easily come to look
upon the phenomenal realm in much the same way as
the Platonist does. What differentiates them is not their
attitudes to the phenomenal realm itself, but the direction in which they severally move from it when they
seek the divine reality. The pantheist will seek to penetrate the phenomenal realm to reach the divine depths
which are beneath it; the Platonist will turn away from
it and seek to soar into the divine heights which are
above it. To use the inevitable spatial metaphors, the
pantheist's god will be *within* the natural world, the
Platonist's god will be *above* it. Mystics of the two types
will devise entirely different techniques, which reach
their typical expressions in such figures as Richard
Jefferies and Plotinus respectively. This is why it seems
to me to be very misleading when some writers, such as
Père Maréchal,[1] apply the word 'pantheism' to the neo-
Platonism of Plotinus; although it conceives creation in
terms of emanation rather than of creative will, it postu-

[1] *Studies in the Psychology of the Mystics*, p. 296.

lates such a radical diversity between the everyday world and the supra-intelligible One which is the object of the mystical ecstasy, that the term 'pantheism' seems totally inapplicable. However, in so far as it attributes some sort of divinity to the human soul, however far that divinity falls short of the supreme divinity of the supra-intelligible One, the system of Plotinus ought perhaps to be placed in the third main division of my table, which I shall now proceed to define. At the moment I will merely add that, just because of their practically identical attitudes to the commonplace phenomenal world, the pantheist and the Platonic types of mysticism, in spite of their theoretical opposition, can easily topple over into each other.

In my tabular statement, parallel with the two main divisions which I have already discussed, I have placed a third main division, containing what I have described as a 'mixed type' of view. Views of this third type drive a sharp wedge between the human soul and the rest of the world, agreeing with the first view as regards the human soul and with the second view as regards the world outside it. That is to say, they look upon the human soul as an independent reality, as in fact divine, and upon the external world as unreal and phantasmal. As in the previous cases there are many qualifications that need to be made. Anyone who asserts that the soul is divine has to meet two obvious objections. One is that the levels of the soul of which we are normally aware— what roughly corresponds to Kant's phenomenal self or to the 'consciousness', as contrasted with the subconscious, of modern psychology—do not seem to be the sort of thing of which divinity can be asserted. The other objection is that there are a great many human souls, whereas people who hold this type of view are usually unwilling to say that there are a large number of gods. In consequence, that of which divinity tends to be asserted is neither the phenomenal self nor the individual self, but a universal human soul, of which the individual selves are assumed to be particularizations, and their phenomenal activities to be manifestations. The phenomenal self of the individual man may very well be looked upon as being unreal and dependent, as in the second type of view, but that upon which it is considered to be dependent is not, as in the second type, a transcendent ideal realm but an immanent energy or principle within the individual soul. The religion to which this third type of view will give rise will thus seek its object neither within the natural world nor above it, but within the human soul. The mystic of this kind will turn away from the sensible world as the Platonist does; but he will not follow the Platonist into the transcendent realm of ideas. On the contrary, he will retreat into his own soul, and in this respect his religion will be more immanentist than that of the pantheistic nature-mystic. The Hinduism of the Upanishads would seem to be of this third anthropotheistic type, but Hinduism is a very complex thing, which we shall have to discuss in some detail. All that has been said before about instability will apply with perhaps even greater relevance to the present case. And it is perhaps important to remark at this point that the

Platonic tradition seems, as I have already assumed, to belong to the second and not to the third type of view in my classification, in spite of the way in which it likes to describe the human soul as divine. For in Platonism, as in the Greek outlook generally, the divinity of the soul does not imply that it is the object of contemplation, but that it is the subject. The object of contemplation, the divine in the *religious* sense, is the realm of ideas, the idea of the Good, the truths of mathematics, or the Plotinian *One*.

2. THEOLOGICAL DOCTRINES AND RELIGIOUS TECHNIQUES

It will be convenient to summarize the above discussion before we make some practical applications of it. Our starting-point was the assertion that the Christian religion holds the world to be real but dependent, and we used these two characteristics of reality and dependence in order to classify the various possible attitudes to the world and to see the kinds of religious techniques to which they would naturally give rise. Clearly, four possible combinations are conceivable. The world might be either (A) real and dependent, or (B) unreal and independent, or (C) real and independent, or (D) unreal and dependent. Alternative A is the doctrine of Judaism and Christianity, though pre-Christian Judaism, which was thoroughly unmetaphysical in outlook, never gave it a coherent philosophical formulation. I remarked that the combination of reality and dependence is by no means easy to conceive, and I suggested that this fact accounts for the prevalence in human history of other views which are superficially less difficult. Alternative B is not, I think, intelligible and I certainly do not know of an instance of it. Alternatives C and D are, on the other hand, very common indeed; the first two main divisions of my tabular summary correspond to them respectively, while its third main division corresponds to a peculiar combination of them both. It may be useful to repeat the scheme, indicating the type of religious technique that is conformable to each.

1. Views of the world as real and independent:
    (i) Atheistic, naturalistic and pluralistic. God does not exist. No religion, though perhaps substitutes for one.
    (ii) Pantheistic and monistic.
        God is *around* us. Nature-mysticism.
2. Views of the world as dependent and unreal. God is *above* us. Platonic (more typically neo-Platonic) mysticism.
3. Views of the external world as dependent and unreal, but the human soul real and independent. God is *within* us. Hinduism, in general.

One further remark may be added at this point, to complicate what is already sufficiently complicated. Pantheist mysticism need not necessarily be nature-mysticism, nor need the mysticism that seeks the divine within the human soul necessarily look upon the external world as unreal. A mystic may conceivably look upon the whole world, including himself, as divine and yet seek the divine not in the external world but in the depths of his own soul, in the belief that the latter is more accessible to him. In practice this is, I think, likely to be a rare case, for the simple reason that the technique of nature-mysticism seems to be easier than the technique of introspection. The fact that we are nearer to ourselves than we are to other beings does not mean that we can contemplate ourselves more easily than we can contemplate them. Few people are likely to seek for the divine in the depths of their own souls if they believe that they can find it equally well in the world around them. But there seems to be no reason in principle why an introspective mysticism should not develop within a pantheistic system.

It should be interesting to see how the foregoing considerations work out when we apply them to the great world-religions. As regards the religion of Islam there is not very much to say at the moment, though there will be a good deal more when we come, in our last chapter, to discuss how the human soul is transformed by union with God. Islam is, on the whole, as clear as Christianity is that the world is a dependent reality, for Islam is radically Semitic in its outlook and, moreover, being the one great religion that is post-Christian in origin, it has been influenced by both Judaism and Christianity. It is, however, worth while noting what happened when the great Arab philosophers of the Middle Ages tried to express the teaching of the Koran in the medium of Aristotelian philosophy. The great Moslem philosopher of the Eastern group, Ibn Sina or Avicenna, an Iranian by birth who lived from A.D. 980

to 1037, while teaching that the world is dependent upon God, held this dependence to be a necessary one.

> A particular object in the world is not necessary of itself: its essence does not involve existence necessarily, as is shown by the fact that it comes into being and passes away; but it is necessary in the sense that its existence is determined by the necessary action of an external cause. . . . A contingent being means, for Avicenna, a being the existence of which is due, not to the essence of the being itself, but to the necessary action of an external cause. Such beings are indeed caused and so 'contingent', but none the less the action of the cause is determined.[1]

And the first cause in the order of necessary causation is God.

The similarity of this system to that of Plotinus in its fundamental necessitarianism will be obvious, and like that of Plotinus it has been described as pantheistic. Nevertheless, as Fr. Copleston remarks:

> Though [Avicenna's] analysis and explanation of creation and the relation of the world to God necessarily involved a theory of emanation and, in this respect, tended towards pantheism, he tried to safeguard himself from pantheism by affirming the distinction between essence and existence in all beings which proceed, immediately or mediately, from God. Possibly the Islamic doctrine of the divine omnipotence, when interpreted 'speculatively', tends to pantheism, and it may well be that some fundamental principles of Avicenna's system would favour pantheism; but he was certainly no pantheist by intention.[2]

[1] F. Copleston, *A History of Philosophy*, II, p. 191.
[2] ibid., p. 194.

It needs, in fact, to be made clear that emanationism as such does not imply pantheism; it all depends upon whether the stuff that emanates from the deity is held to be divine or not. On the other hand, a deity who is bound to create, and to create one particular world with one particular set of characteristics, clearly has not the kind of independence and supremacy that belong to a God who is free to create or not as he wills and in what way he wills; and we can hardly be surprised that Avicenna found it difficult to reconcile his doctrines with strict Koranic orthodoxy. Still less are they compatible with Christian theism. To quote M. Étienne Gilson:

> In order to become assimilable later on to Christian thought, Avicenna's universe will have to admit at its origin the decision of a supremely free divine will. This radical metamorphosis, which was to transform Avicenna's hierarchical ladder of conditioned necessities into a vast contingency, was to be the work of Duns Scotus.[1]

But in Islam itself the necessitarianism of Avicenna was attacked by such outstanding thinkers as Algazel and Averroes, and, although Averroes incurred the hostility of the Islamic theologians for his tendency to subordinate theology to philosophy, there does not seem to be very much amiss with his doctrine of the relation of the world to its Creator.

In sharp contrast with the transcendentalism of Islam there stands the immanentist monism of Hinduism. The earliest of the Hindu scriptures, the *Rig Veda*, which is a collection of over a thousand hymns, is, on the whole,

---

[1] *La Philosophie au Moyen Age*, 2nd ed., p. 354.

frankly polytheistic. By the fifth century B.C., however, Indian religion seems to have decided upon the course it was going to follow. In the *Rig Veda* itself a sceptical note is apparent and one of the best known of its hymns ends with the words:

> He, the first origin of this creation, whether he formed
>   it all or did not form it,
> Whose eye controls this world in highest heaven, he
>   verily knows it, or perhaps he knows not.[1]

'Balancing the scepticism', it has been said, 'there was a feeling after unity, but instead of seeking it in one God and his moral law, they sought it in one physical life running through all things, so taking the first steps towards worship of the All and away from the living and forgiving God. . . . The turning, once taken, led these Aryans very far.'[2] The great body of philosophical and religious treatises which are known as the *Upanishads* are permeated by a doctrine of immanentist monism, according to which the fundamental Reality, the One or *Brahman* is identical with the *Atman*, the Self. This doctrine can take a great variety of forms and there are many disparate theories within Hinduism, but they tend to converge in seeking the object of religious contemplation neither in the world of nature nor in a suprasensible ideal world, but in the depths of the human soul. Perhaps the most typical interpretation of the teaching of the Upanishads is provided by the monist Vedantism of Sankara, who lived in the eighth century A.D. He

---

[1] 'The Song of Creation', *Rig Veda*, X, 129.
[2] G. E. Phillips, *The Religions of the World*, pp. 49, 50.

taught an uncompromising monism, a doctrine of non-duality (*advaita*); only Brahman is real, and beatitude consists in grasping the unity of one's self in its fundamental identity with Brahman. At first sight, we might suppose this to be a pantheist or, if the word 'pantheist' has too personal a ring, a *panhenist* doctrine—everything is really the same. We might expect it to issue in some form of nature-worship or nature-mysticism, since if everything is really divine, whatever we worship we shall be worshipping divinity. In point of fact, the exact opposite is the case: and we get a religion of extreme introversion. For if everything that exists is divine or eternal, and the divine or eternal excludes all multiplicity and mutability, then everything that is multiple and mutable is automatically excluded from existence. Neither the phenomenal world of nature nor the psychophysical ratiocinating self can find a place in reality; both are dismissed as illusion, *maya*. All that is real is the changeless consciousness in which the soul is identical with Brahman; and the Vedanta defines Brahman in the phrase *sat-at-ananda*, 'being-consciousness-joy'.

To a modern Western positivist philosopher all this will seem to be merely verbal nonsense. You cannot (he will protest) simply argue the empirical world away. Whether or not the world exists in some unnatural and esoteric sense of 'exist', in which existence is synonymous with some equally fantastic and unverifiable notion of 'divinity', in the ordinary everyday sense of the word 'existence' the phenomenal world goes on existing just as if

Sankara had never been heard of. This is, of course, perfectly true, but it does not settle the matter with which we are concerned. For what the Hindu mystic means by existence or reality is not mere sensible perceptibility; he means permanence and supreme value. He is not concerned with finding visual and tangible objects, but with attaining beatitude. And what the doctrine of *advaita* and *maya* means from this point of view is that the way to beatitude consists of an introverted psychological simplification. This is admirably summarized in the following words of Père Maréchal:

Experience, it will be replied, sets before me unquestionably the multiplicity of objects. True, but that multiplicity has no real existence, it is only apparent, an illusion, Maya; it is, in my mind, the veil of the Absolute, the manifold refraction of the One. My destiny, if I do not resign myself to gravitate in the endless becoming of ignorance, is, therefore, to extirpate in myself the illusory multiplicity of objects and acts, and to retire within the Atman, the absolute Unity that I am. Shall I then know the Atman? Yes and no; I shall not know it objectively, for that would mean the continued maintenance of the duality of subject and object; but I shall have become the Atman, and the Atman is its own light; I shall have become Brahman, and beyond that there is nothing.

Summary as they are, these few lines define one kind of mysticism. By destroying the illusion of phenomena, and reducing in myself the multiplicity of representations and of acts, I wholly blot out the universe and the limitations of my *ego*; but by so doing I conquer myself, I become what I am, the Absolute. A mysticism negative in its psychological processes . . . but positive in the fundamental orientation of its development.[1]

It is in this way that we must understand the well-known formula *Tat tvam asi*, 'That art thou'. It must be admitted that some other Hindu teachers are less ruthless in their monism than is Sankara; thus Ramanuja, nearly three centuries later, developed a doctrine of distinctions within unity which comes at some points so close to Christian doctrine that he has sometimes been supposed, in spite of the lack of positive evidence, to have borrowed some of his ideas from Christianity. For Ramanuja a personal God really exists and is not, as for Sankara, part of the realm of illusion, *maya*. Furthermore, the individual soul is real and indestructible, and an attempt is made to distinguish it, as a real existent, from the mere idea of it in the mind of God. Nevertheless, fettered as he is by the fundamental monism of the Upanishads, Ramanuja does not seem to do more than approximate to the clear and confident conviction of the Christian tradition that both man and the world which his senses display to him are real, though dependent, beings, drawing their existence and their activity from the free creative fiat of an omnipotent personal God. There may perhaps be room for doubt, if indeed one can validly generalize about something so protean as Hinduism, whether in my tabular statement it ought not to have been placed in section 1 (ii) rather than in section 3, where I have actually placed it. What has, however, finally determined my location of it is the fact that the

[1] Op. cit., p. 295.

religion to which it gives rise is almost entirely of the introverted and not of the nature-mysticism type.

It will be interesting to compare with the intransigeant monism of Sankara and the mitigated monism of Ramanuja the very different system of Hindu thought which goes by the name of *Sankhya* and whose traditional founder was Kapila, who lived in or before the sixth century B.C. It seems likely indeed that the Sankhya system originated in a reaction against the monism of the Upanishads, but that it established its position by claiming to provide their true interpretation. It is frankly naturalistic and atheistic. It believes that the world of our experience is the only reality that there is, and it divides the stuff of which the world is made into two essentially different types of being, matter or *prakrati* and the soul or *purusha*. Matter is fundamentally mutable and is the seat of all process and change; it is not in itself unpleasant or evil, but our whole hope of beatitude consists in the possibility of getting free from it. In this process of disentanglement matter itself may co-operate. The way to liberation is a complete detachment of *purusha* from *prakrati* by turning from the external world into the depths of the soul, and the ultimate state of beatitude will be one in which all concern with change and matter has ceased in a blissful self-consciousness. Theoretically, then, the Sankhya doctrine ought to come in section 1 of our table, as a form of naturalistic and pluralistic atheism. In practice, however, it comes to much the same thing as the doctrine of Sankara, and this lends some speciousness to its claim to be a genuine interpretation of Hinduism. For they both agree in their radically negative attitude to the phenomenal world and in their technique of introversion. The Sankhya pluralism flees from the external world as an agreeable but embarrassing reality, the Vedantist monism flees from it as a horrid illusion. And both of them see beatitude as the escape from change and multiplicity into undifferentiated unity. Resting upon very different theoretical bases, they both issue in an introverted spirituality which renounces the world of normal changing experience. It must, however, be recognized that what they seek in the depths of the soul is not the same; the Vedantist mystic is seeking the eternal ground of all existence, the Sankhya mystic is seeking sheer isolation. How the God in whom Christianity believes may show himself to those who, however perversely, seek in good faith for the supreme good it is not for us to say, but there can be no doubt as to the judgment that a Christian must pass upon these techniques considered as such. It is that neither of them is in fact directed towards the liberation of the soul by union with God, but rather to the folding in of the soul upon itself. It is hardly surprising that Gautama Buddha took the one step that remained in the direction in which the Sankhya system was pointing, and elaborated a technique by which the soul might escape from misery by escaping from existence altogether, or, if a total escape from existence was impossible —and on this point there does not seem to be agreement among Buddhists themselves—by what would for practical purposes do just as well, namely the attainment of complete indifference as to whether one continued to exist or not. There are few human characters as appealing as Gautama Buddha, as the Buddhist scriptures depict him, with his yearning to deliver his fellow-men from the misery in which he sees them entangled and his determination not to achieve his own liberation until he has laid down the Noble Path by which they may attain theirs; but there is no metaphysical system so radically opposed to Christianity as is that of Buddhism, with its unqualified abhorrence of a world which to the Christian is the work of omnipotent and personal love.[1]

[1] It is only right to add that a certain number of students in recent years have denied that Hindu thought at its most authentic is really pantheistic; reference may be made to two articles by Victor White, O.P., and Bernard Kelly in *Dominican Studies* for 1954 and to *The Quintessence of Hinduism* by H. O. Mascarenhas, an Indian Roman Catholic priest. By these writers the accusation of pantheism is alleged to rest upon a misunderstanding. If they are correct, the 'identity' of God with creatures in Hinduism means nothing more than the Thomist doctrines that in the order of exemplary causality all creatures are identical with God as ideas in the divine mind and that God is in all his creatures 'by essence, presence and power'. The relation between God and creatures is conceived as a 'principial' relation. Fr. Mascarenhas writes as follows:
'Taken dependently, the universe of manifestation because of its intrinsic limitation and this very entitative *dependence* can never stand comparison metaphysically with the Infinitude of the Supreme Principle, which holds all actual and possible manifestations *principially*. . . .
'*Principial* relations are not simple relations and can allow perfect *identity in principle*, while affirming the transcendence of the Infinite in a manner that can leave no intelligent person in doubt. *Principial* relations are neither convertible nor reversible, and every suggestion of "pantheism" or "immanentism" is cut at the root' (op. cit., pp. 64–5).
Again Fr. Victor White writes, with reference to reincarnation:
'More attention could be paid, both by orientalists and by Chris-

As we have seen, very similar religious techniques may arise from very different metaphysical doctrines. You may seek beatitude in the depths of your soul because you believe that you are God and nature is not, or because you believe that nature is God and you are part of it, or because you believe that there is no God anywhere and you want to be alone. Again you may try to achieve union with nature because you believe it is God, or because you believe that there is no God but nature is the only reality that there is. And even a spirituality which professes to be atheistic may well end up by applying the terms of theism to whatever object it seeks as its goal. You may begin by denying that God exists and seek your beatitude in some other object, and end by calling this object God because you are seeking your beatitude in it. The study of human religion is beset with linguistic pitfalls of this kind, and over and above all there is the fact upon which I have repeatedly in-

tians, to Coomaraswamy's study on the subject. This great scholar contended that what he calls the 'animistic' view of reincarnation is a distortion of the authentic oriental tradition, and that Sankara's doctrine that "In truth, there is no other Transmigrator but the Lord" (*Brahma Sutra*, I, 1, 5) represents the original tradition of the Vedas and Upanishads. With such a tradition informed Christians could have no quarrel. Such a doctrine would, indeed, be an unfolding of the implications of Christian tradition itself. For according to it, it would not be the individual soul, life or *jiva* which transmigrates, but the immortal, omnipresent and indwelling God: an assertion which Christians should also affirm' (art. cit., p. 3).

Clearly, everything turns upon whether the universe is believed to proceed from God by an act of the divine will or by a quasi-physical necessity; this is a point to which none of the writers mentioned seems to have given attention.

sisted, of the essential instability of non-Christian religions, the enantiodromia by which any of the positions may without warning transform itself into its opposite. This instability, we may remark, will be interpreted by a Christian as a sign of the inherent inadequacy of the non-Christian doctrines to give an accurate account of the world which they profess to describe.

3. CREATION AND ITS IMPLICATIONS

Having discussed at some length the various alternatives to the Christian doctrine of creation, we must now pay a little more attention to the Christian doctrine itself, the doctrine of the world as dependent reality. One or two preliminary remarks need to be made. In the first place, we are not directly concerned with the question whether the world had a temporal beginning. Therefore we are still less concerned with the question of the extent to which the narratives of the early chapters of the book Genesis are to be interpreted symbolically. It is, of course, true that these narratives are frequently described as 'creation-stories' and that Christian tradition has generally taken them as implying that the world has not existed for an infinite time in the past. Nevertheless, when philosophical theology speaks of the world as created it is not making an assertion about an event which is alleged to have taken place at some date in remote antiquity; it is making an assertion about a characteristic which is alleged to apply to the world at every moment of its existence. We may remember that

St. Thomas Aquinas scandalized many of his contemporaries by the tenacity with which he argued that, apart from the testimony of divine revelation, it would be impossible to know whether the world had an infinite past duration or not; in either case, he held, the world is rightly described as 'created', since it depends for its existence from moment to moment upon the creative will of God.[1] Some modern scholastics have indeed gone so far as to maintain that, in the case of finite beings, the act of existence does not merely *imply* dependence upon God but is flatly identical with it. This point of view has been vigorously argued by Dom Mark Pontifex and Dom Illtyd Trethowan in their book *The Meaning of Existence*.[2] They remark that, while existence is a common characteristic of all finite beings, it cannot be a constituent of their nature, since the nature of any one of them would be precisely the same whether it existed or not. What then, they ask, can this characteristic be which applies to every one of them, but belongs to the nature of none of them? It can, they reply, only be their common aspect of derivation from a single source, their relation of dependence upon God. Hence, when we apprehend the existence of any object in its full ontological force, when, that is, we have learnt *to see the object as it really is*, we simultaneously, although mediately, apprehend its creative cause, God. As Dom Pontifex has said elsewhere, the direct object of our knowledge is *effect-implying-cause*.[3] It is in this way, and not as in-

---

[1] *S. Theol.*, I, xliv–xlvi; *S.c.G.*, II, xvi, xvii, xxxii–xxxviii.
[2] Ch. i.   [3] *The Existence of God*, p. 31.

volving any syllogistic argumentation, that Pontifex and Trethowan understand the cosmological approach to theism, that is to say, the approach which takes as its starting-point the existence of the finite world. And other writers, such as Dr. Farrer and myself,[1] who would hesitate to regard finite existence and dependence upon God as *logically identical*, have also maintained that the basis of the cosmological approach is what may be called a *contuition*[2] of God in the apprehension of finite beings, or, in Dr. Farrer's term, the apprehension of 'the "cosmological idea"—the scheme of God and the creature in relation'.[3] For if theism is true—if the very heart and root of creaturehood is dependence upon God —then, if we perceive creatures as they really are, we shall perceive them as dependent upon God, and so we shall recognize God as him upon whom they are dependent. Why we so often fail to do so is a question to which I shall shortly return. We have already digressed sufficiently from the point at which we began, namely that creation in the philosophical sense is not concerned with an alleged beginning of the world at some epoch in the past.

A further point, which is related to the above, is that creation has no material cause, in the Aristotelian sense

---

[1] A. M. Farrer, *Finite and Infinite*; E. L. Mascall, *He Who Is* and *Existence and Analogy*.

[2] I take this term, which is defined as 'the apprehension of the presence of the cause in a perceived effect', from the discussion of St. Bonaventure in *Mediaeval Mystical Tradition and St. John of the Cross*, by a Benedictine of Stanbrook, p. 70.

[3] Op. cit., p. 16.

of that phrase. Creation is not, as it was conceived to be in the myth of Plato's *Timaeus*, the manipulation of pre-existent material by a divine craftsman. We speak of God making the world out of nothing, but this must not be taken as meaning that nothing is something out of which God makes the world. What we mean is that God makes the world, but does not make it out of anything. And this will bring us to the main point with which we are now concerned, namely that creation is not to be looked upon as any kind of process or change, however naturally we tend to picture it in this way, but as being, from the side of the creature, *a pure relation of dependence*. We must never allow ourselves to think of creation as if it were a kind of intermediary between God and the world. The notion of intermediaries between God and the world is a thoroughly pagan notion, and, as the history of the Church's struggle against gnosticism and Arianism shows, its extermination was one of the most urgent and troublesome tasks which Christianity had to perform as soon as it faced the dangerous but necessary undertaking of translating the message of the Bible into the mental language of Greco-Roman thought. We tend to think of God and creation and the world as three realities, each of which, except the first, derives from the one before, but such a thought, however useful for some purposes, is an abstraction and a dangerous one at that. For creation (in the sense of the creative *act*) does not *exist* at all; all that exists is God on the one hand, in complete self-sufficiency, and the creature on the other, in pure dependence. This 'creation', which we so easily hypostatize, is a pure abstraction, whose sole function is to express the fact that creatures, existing in pure dependence, exist in pure dependence upon the will of God.

This is not the place for a full discussion of this unique and highly paradoxical notion of creation or of the many problems to which it gives rise; I have discussed some of them in the chapter on 'God and the Creature' in my book *Existence and Analogy*. I shall merely repeat from that discussion some words of Père Sertillanges which put the essential point as clearly as any summary that I know.

> From the side of God, no effect arises from the fact that the world exists. From the side of the creature, too, no effect arises, except the creature itself and the relation of dependence which it has to its primary Source. Now see what follows. In order for the creature to be in relation with God it must first of all exist. If creation is this relation, then creation comes into the order of being after the creature. This is indeed turning the world upside down! Nevertheless, it is so; it cannot but be so, once it is admitted that absolutely nothing is interposed between God, who is the world's cause, and the world as it begins; that the world is prior in time, with its quality of being a dependent thing, and that this attribute, which is creation itself, is necessarily subsequent, both for our minds and in the nature of things (*intellectu et natura*, as St. Thomas says), to the subject which it relates to its creator.[1]

It is important to emphasize how thoroughly positive and exhilarating is this doctrine that the world is a de-

[1] *L'Idée de Création*, p. 46.

pendent reality. From time to time a tendency appears, even within Christendom itself, to suppose that in order to give glory to God it is necessary to hold his creatures in contempt, and to assert as the fundamental fact about the world that, apart from the creative activity of God, it would be nothing. It is, of course, true that, apart from the creative activity of God the world would be nothing, but this is not the fundamental fact about it. The fundamental fact about it is that, under the creative activity of God, it is precisely what it is; it is a dependent reality which manifests on the finite level a limited but none the less genuine expression of the goodness and beauty which exists in its unlimited archetypal mode in God himself. Once again, I shall quote some words of Sertillanges:

> That beings tend to non-being taken literally has no meaning; for non-being, not being anything, cannot be the object of a tendency. Anything that *is* tends to *being*, and not only to being but to the perfection of its being. . . . To realize the creative thought is indeed our whole ideal . . .
>
> The tendency of every creature to persevere in being is a reality, but this tendency does not come from its own sole power, it comes from the Cause from which it derives its being; as, on the other hand, if we say that it tends to non-being, this is not because of its nature but because of its deficiency . . .
>
> Let us repeat once for all, with careful attention to every word: creatures, as soon as they exist, tend to exist and not to collapse. But first of all they must exist. Now they do not exist of themselves. And thus the power that they need is not one which would prevent them from collapsing when

they existed, but one which makes them exist. The point of application of this power is not between the creatures and an alleged non-being, thought of as a kind of chasm; Henri Bergson has once for all exorcised this image in a famous piece of analysis. [The reference is presumably to the beginning of chapter iv of *L'Évolution Créatrice*.] The point of application of the sustaining power is between the creatures and God, in order that the contact shall not be broken and that the creature shall continue to flow from its source.[1]

As I have written elsewhere:

No more radical distinction could be found than that between God and his creatures, nor (at least if we restrict ourselves to the realm of natural theology) any more intimate relation than that in which they are united to him in their creation. And these two facts—the fact of distinction and the fact of the relation—are only two aspects of the one fundamental cosmological truth, the truth of finite being as genuinely existing and yet existing with an existence that is altogether derived.[2]

It is this fundamental truth, namely that, for all finite beings, to exist is to derive reality from the creative will of God, which makes it possible for us to believe that there is such a study as natural theology. It is, of course, well known that in many quarters in recent years the whole notion of natural or rational theology has been denounced as illegitimate, and it has been asserted that the only knowledge of God which is possible to man

[1] Op. cit., p. 68. The passage is quoted in full in my *Existence and Analogy*, p. 147.
[2] *Existence and Analogy*, p. 148.

comes from specific revelatory acts, and in particular from the act in which God reveals himself in Jesus Christ. The controversy between Barth and Brunner which began in 1934 cannot yet be considered as ended,[1] though it has tended to concern itself not so much with the possibility of natural theology—a possibility which both the protagonists professed to deny—as with the question whether, in spite of his denials, Brunner really believes in natural theology after all. Neither the protagonists themselves nor their disciples seem to have succeeded in completely avoiding confusion, and it is necessary to make some careful distinctions if the issues are to be clear.

We may in the first place notice that many theologians who have little in common with the thought of neo-Protestantism have objected to the traditional distinction between reason and revelation in theology. Thus the late Dr. William Temple in his Gifford Lectures insisted that the alleged data of revelation itself were legitimate matter for rational investigation.[2] On the other hand, Dr. Leonard Hodgson and the late Dr. O. C. Quick have questioned the distinction upon the very different, though not contradictory, ground that, since God is a personal being, he never offers himself as a purely passive object to our examination and that therefore all our knowledge of God, as the self-disclosure

---

[1] Brunner's essay *Natur und Gnade* and Barth's reply *Nein!* were published together in an English translation in 1946 under the title *Natural Theology*.

[2] *Nature, Man and God*, ch. i.

of a personal being, is rightly to be described as 'revealed'.[1] In so far as some traditional scholastics may
have interpreted the terms 'natural theology' or 'rational
theology' as implying that the living God can be made
the unresisting object of a rational inquisition, we may
well be grateful for the warning. It is not here that the
point of controversy with the neo-Protestants arises. As
Dr. Farrer pointed out in his Bampton Lectures,
' "Reason and Revelation" is a current description, but
a bad description, for the antithesis which we have to
discuss. We ought to say "*Natural* Reason and *Supernatural* Revelation", and we ought to throw the emphasis on the adjectives rather than upon the nouns. We
have not to distinguish between God's action and ours,
but between two phases of God's action—his supernatural action, and his action by way of nature.'[2] The
point of issue between the general tradition of Catholic
philosophy and the neo-Protestants is not whether God
is known to us in nature as a purely passive object—that
we can all deny—but whether God makes himself known
to us in nature and through our reason at all. It is this
last assertion that neo-Protestants are so vehement in
rejecting, though it must be recognized that their
grounds for rejecting it are very varied.

Thus, for example, Brunner writes as follows:

It is important to know two things: first, that from the
very beginning God has revealed himself in his creation, but

[1] L. Hodgson, *The Doctrine of the Trinity*, p. 15f.; O. C. Quick,
Doctrines of the Creed, p. 9f.
[2] A. M. Farrer, *The Glass of Vision*, p. 3.

that we can only know what this means through his revelation in Jesus Christ; and to know that we men, from the very beginning, have been created in and for this Image of God, and that no sin of ours can destroy this original destiny of human nature. Secondly, it is equally important to realise that it is only in Jesus Christ that we know our original destiny, and that it is only through him that this 'Image' is realised in us.[1]

This is not, of course, the traditional view of Catholicism, but it is a comparatively mild form of Protestant view. It looks upon the created order as capable of providing a real, even if limited and incomplete, manifestation of God, and it attributes the *de facto* perversity of human religion at least as much to man's sinfulness as to his creaturehood. In Karl Barth, on the other hand, the denial of natural theology rests upon what can only be described as a metaphysical basis. It is not primarily because he is *sinful* that man cannot see God in nature; to assert that would itself be an example of the sinful perversity of man. The very notion of *analogia entis*—the notion that created beings are, in virtue of their creaturehood, able either to manifest or to apprehend the activity of God—is denounced as one of the basic errors of Catholicism and as itself an indication of man's radical inability to know God's truth. Creation as such sets up no point of contact between the creature and its Creator. It is only when God addresses himself to man in revelatory acts which are subsequent to creation that man can apprehend him, and then only because, with the revela-

[1] *Dogmatics*, I, p. 21.

tory act, God bestows the power to recognize and to understand it.[1] 'The possibility of a knowledge of God's Word lies in God's Word and nowhere else.'[2] In place of the *analogia entis* of Catholic theology, which is denounced with the utmost vigour, there is simply an *analogia fidei*.[3] 'That the faith, in which the true God is believed, is true faith, is something which is due . . . in no way and in no sense to itself, but to the fact that the true God has revealed himself to it.'[4] It seems to be clear that Barth does not hold that man's inability to know God through creation is due simply to the impoverishment and perversion which have overcome man's perceptivity as a result of the Fall; though he would, no doubt, admit that the Fall has made man even blinder than he would have been by nature. On the contrary, he would maintain that the holding of such a view is an effect and a sign of man's corruption; that fallen man has an unduly roseate view not only of his fallen, but also of his unfallen, state. The very existence of something which calls itself natural theology is 'the perfect expression of man's enmity to grace'.[5] There is nothing either in man's own constitution or in the constitution of the natural world which can serve as a point of contact for God's communication of himself to man. Man can apprehend God only when God addresses a word to him and at the same time communicates the

---

[1] Cf. O. Weber, *Karl Barth's Church Dogmatics*, ch. vi. Barth himself has certified that this book gives an accurate account of his teaching.
[2] Ibid., p. 30.   [3] Ibid., p. 31.   [4] Ibid., p. 30.   [5] Ibid., p. 79.

power to hear it. Such a doctrine of revelation as this seems to deny all significance to the creature as such. Barth would, of course, assert that finite beings are altogether dependent upon God for their existence and their nature; but, for him, this fact no more enables God to be approached or discerned through them than if they had no connection with him at all. Metaphysically they may be dependent realities, but noetically they are sheer barriers behind which man cannot penetrate. It is impossible not to feel that there is something doctrinaire about this radical opposition between the order of being and the order of knowledge, and that Barth has fallen a victim to his passion for startling his hearers by rhetoric and exaggeration. He seems in fact to be hag-ridden by his fear that natural theology must inevitably treat God as impersonal. We must recall Dr. Farrer's insistence that the contrast between natural and revealed theology is not the contrast between purely human ratiocination and divine self-manifestation, but between the natural and the supernatural self-communication of God. What natural theology is in fact asserting is that God is not to be found solely in disconnected and arbitrary acts but also in the continuous activity by which he preserves and energizes the dependent reality which is the finite world, and that in so far as man is able to recognize the finite world as what it really is, he is able to recognize its Creator. This does not of course mean that in his actual condition man is easily able to recognize either the true nature of the world or the God upon whom it depends; indeed all the earlier part of this chapter was devoted to a detailed exposition of the way in which human religions in general have failed to do this. *De facto*, fallen man's capacity to enter into personal relations with God through his creation is extremely clouded and distorted, and it may well need special graces from God if man is to recognize and respond to him who is the ground of both man's existence and the existence of the world. This does not affect the point that, since the world is God's creation, it is *in principle* possible for God to speak to man through it and for man to hear God's voice. That is the fundamental claim, and the only necessary claim, of natural theology. But we may observe that, besides the obscuration of man's mind by sin, there is a further fact, and indeed a somewhat paradoxical fact, which co-operates with this obscuration to hamper man's recognition of God in nature.

God's very generosity to his creatures can prevent our clouded and weak vision from recognizing him as their Creator. If he had given them less than he has given them, we should recognize him more easily. If he had made a world which was not dependent and real but dependent and *unreal*, that is to say if he had surrounded us with unsubstantial phantom forms which half concealed and half revealed the divine activity within them, if they had no substantiality, no autonomy, not even a relative spontaneity, but were purely phenomenal media for the manifestation to us of the absolute autonomy and primary causality of God, then we could hardly help perceiving God when we directed our gaze towards them. Just as when we look through a microscope we see not the lens-system of the microscope but the object upon which it is focused, so in this case when we looked at creatures we should see not the creatures but the God who was their origin. God has, however, given his world more reality than this. His creatures are real beings, although their reality is dependent and communicated. It is therefore hardly surprising that our weakened and misdirected sight can only too easily recognize the reality and ignore the dependence. For it would hardly be an exaggeration to say that God has given his creatures everything that he himself has except self-existence. We could hardly mistake them for the ultimate reality unless they were undeniably real. This is, I think, at least one reason for the fact upon which Dr. C. S. Lewis has commented, that the human mind, as we see it in history, has a persistent tendency to fall into pantheism.

So far from being the final religious refinement [he writes], pantheism is in fact the permanent natural bent of the human mind; the permanent ordinary level below which man sometimes sinks, under the influence of priestcraft and superstition, but above which his own unaided efforts can never raise him for very long. Platonism and Judaism, and Christianity (which has incorporated both) have proved the only things capable of resisting it. It is the attitude into which the human mind automatically falls when left to itself.[1]

But we ought perhaps to add that, when a civilization has become radically desupernaturalized in its outlook,

[1] *Miracles*, p. 101.

as has the western industrialized civilization to which we belong, this inability to see beyond the creature to the Creator will usually take the form, not of pantheism, but of sheer atheistic naturalism. The world is accepted as the ultimate reality, but that ultimate reality is not conceived as divine.

There is, we may observe at this point, one particularly stubborn theological problem which it is impossible to discuss at all profitably if one has failed to grasp in its full meaning the fact that the finite world is a dependent reality; I mean the problem of the relation of the primary causality of God to the secondary causality of creatures. The problem becomes particularly acute when the creatures in question are rational beings, who at least seem to possess the power to determine their own actions, and it arises on both the natural and the supernatural level. On the natural level it is the problem of reconciling human freedom with divine omnipotence; on the supernatural level it is the problem of reconciling human freedom with the fact that we are saved not by our own efforts but by the pure grace of God. The mere recollection of the passionate controversies which have gathered round the names of Augustine, Pelagius, Jansen and Molina will remind us how obstinate the problem is, and how inconclusive and unsatisfactory most of the discussions of it have been; and perhaps the best way to grasp the points at issue is to attend to the dispute between the Thomists and the Molinists in the sixteenth century. In the view of Molina, 'the immediate influence of God's motion takes effect, not on the second cause, so

premoving it to act and to produce its effect, but on the
action and the effect, where it acts side by side with the
second cause; so that God and the second cause are both
partially responsible for the production of the effect,
since they both act on it immediately and simultaneously, "not otherwise than when two drag a ship".[1]
On the other hand, 'the Thomists have always maintained that in order to safeguard the independence and
entire actuality of God, as well as the freedom of human
action, it is necessary to assert that God's motion bears,
not merely on the action and its effect, but also on the
agent as the cause of the action itself, inasmuch as it
applies the agent to act, and causes in it and with it both
the action and its mode, whether this mode be necessary
or free'.[2] To the obvious objection that, on the Thomist
view, the freedom of a rational creature's will is purely
fictitious, the Thomists reply, in agreement with their
master, that God moves all secondary causes in accordance with their nature, moving natural causes in accordance with the nature of natural causes, and voluntary
causes in accordance with the nature of voluntary
causes.[3] To the Molinists, of course, this reply is nothing
but an ingenious quibble, while to the Thomists the
Molinist doctrine deposes God from his sovereignty
over his creation. Both parties to the controversy have,

---

[1] R. P. Phillips, *Modern Thomistic Philosophy*, II, p. 343. The interior quotation is from Molina, *Concordia*, XVI, 13, xxvi.
[2] Ibid.
[3] Cf. *S. Theol.* I, lxxxiii, 1 *ad* 3. In this statement, 'natural' is, of
course, contrasted with 'voluntary', not with 'supernatural'; it simply
indicates the absence of volition.

I think, tended to forget the paradoxical but indisputable fact that when we are dealing with the relation between personal beings (and, however disparate God and man may be, they are both of them personal), the strength of one person's influence upon another is frequently shown not in the suppression of the latter's initiative and autonomy, but in their stimulation and liberation. This is not, however, my present point. What I wish to emphasize at the moment is that the very acuteness and difficulty of the problem arise precisely from the fact that, in contrast with some other systems, orthodox Christianity is committed to the view of man as a dependent reality, in the full sense of this twofold term. If we deny or belittle man's dependence (as I fear the Molinists tend to do), then there is no real problem; man and God are exercising separate powers, and the resultant effect can be calculated from the two in a way analogous to the method of the parallelogram of forces in mechanics. If, on the other hand, we deny or belittle man's reality, again the problem evaporates; man's apparent activity is only an illusion or a fiction, the sole real activity is God's. It is just because man's creaturely status involves this delicately and precariously balanced combination of dependence and reality that both these simple, but also over-simplified, solutions must be rejected. I believe that the Thomist position is right and the Molinist position wrong; not, however, because Thomism gives a clear-cut answer, but because it understands the real nature of the question and therefore refuses to do so. If, as I have suggested, the fundamental mystery about creation is that God creates a world at all, that is to say, that the self-existent Reality wills the existence of dependent realities, there is a mystery at the creature's very heart. We ought not therefore to be surprised if this mystery about the creature's existence is accompanied by a mystery about its operation. Be this as it may, there can be little doubt that the reason why Christianity has throughout its history been so persistently occupied with the problem of reconciling the universality of the primary causality of God with the reality of the secondary causality of his creatures is that it is committed by its doctrine of creation to maintaining in their full force both aspects of the dual notion of the creature as a dependent reality.

There are a number of other questions which might be discussed before leaving this subject. In particular, it might be shown that the very possibility of grace, as Catholic theology understands the term, as a real participation by the creature in the life of God, rests upon the fact that the creature is, by its nature, a dependent reality. And then we might develop the consequences of this in the realm of mystical theology. It will, however, be better to postpone this discussion to the last chapter of this book, in which the doctrine of grace will be considered as such. In concluding the present chapter, I will simply emphasize a point upon which I have already touched, namely that it is only when finite beings are recognized as dependent realities that we can wholeheartedly rejoice in them without danger of idolatry. The Christian attitude to creatures is neither to worship them for their own sake nor, on the other hand, to treat them with contempt in order, by contrast, to extol the glory and perfection of God. Sin has indeed distorted God's world, but in their ontological depth creatures are contrasted with God not by being sinful but being finite. And to pass from the finite to the Infinite, we have not to depress the finite but to surpass it. As a matter of ascetic practice it is, of course, true that we have from time to time to resist the appeal of God's creatures if we are to avoid being seduced by them from our allegiance to God; but in doing this we are passing judgment not upon God's creation but upon our own sinful condition. Fundamentally our attitude to the world must be first to recognize the beauty and loveliness that it embodies even in its fallen state, and then to remind ourselves that even this beauty and loveliness is only the faintest shadow or reflection of the infinite beauty and loveliness of God. *Quo majus*—'How much more'—is the reflection which should lead the human understanding and will not *away from* the creature, but *through* the creature, to God.

> How wonderful creation is,
> The work that thou didst bless,
> And O! what then must thou be like,
> Eternal loveliness?

And there is perhaps no Christian saint who has realized this truth with such vividness and simplicity as St. Francis of Assisi, who, recognizing the glory of the sun and the moon and the flowers and the fire, called upon them to join with him in praising the supreme glory of the Lord who was his creator and theirs.

II

DERIVED EQUALITY
THE DOCTRINE OF THE TRINITY

I. NICENE ORTHODOXY AND THE ALTERNATIVES

When the *Quicunque vult* tells us that 'the Father is God,
the Son is God, and the Holy Ghost is God; and yet
there are not three Gods, but one God', it is summing up
in one succinct and paradoxical sentence the fruits of
three centuries of theological discussion and controversy.
Nevertheless, the truth to which it bears witness was implicit in the religion of Chrstians from the moment when
a young Jewish rabbi, walking by the lakeside in Galilee,
spoke to four working fishermen in accents which they
could not resist and commanded them to follow him.
For the authority which Jesus of Nazareth claimed and
assumed over his followers, and which his followers,
fanatical monotheists as they were by their Jewish
profession, readily, and, as it were, almost unconsciously,
conceded to him, was an authority which could be
rightly claimed and assumed only by God himself. His
enemies at least had no illusions on this point when they
alleged that the unique sense in which he declared that
God was his father amounted to nothing less than

47

making himself equal to God. It is, I think, only because in the modern world we have lost something of the horror which, in the polytheistic world of their acquaintance, the Jews of the first century felt at the least suggestion of idolatry, that we fail to see the staggering metaphysical implications of the claim to an absolutely unqualified and unconditional allegiance which Jesus made upon his disciples, both in his spoken utterances and—which is even more striking—by the mere impact of his personality. Nor was this impact confined to those who had seen him in the flesh; it was no less strong upon those who had come to know him simply through their membership of his body the Catholic Church. 'Eighty and six years have I served him and he did me no wrong', replied Polycarp of Smyrna to the Roman proconsul who was urging him to save his life by abjuring Christ, 'How can I blaspheme my King that saved me?' And in our own days it has been precisely the claim of the totalitarian systems to an absolute allegiance that has, in one place after another, led the Church to realize that submission would be equivalent to idolatry. Hitler, for example, never called himself God nor did he demand to be accorded religious worship, but the unconditional claims which he made, alike for himself and his régime, were rightly recognized by German Christians to be claims that God alone could rightly make upon men.

The Christian Church was not slow to realize what her attitude to her Lord involved. Dr. Prestige has put it very clearly in his magisterial work *God in Patristic Thought*:

From the earliest moment of theological reflection it was assumed that Jesus Christ was true God as well as true Man. The Adoptionists, such as the elder and younger Theodotus at the end of the second century, who taught that Christ was a mere man, inspired by the Holy Spirit and deified only after his ascension, may have possessed a theological ancestry in certain obscure sects; but both they and their forerunners stand clearly outside the main stream of Christian experience. The problem which the Fathers had to solve was not whether he was God, but how, within the monotheistic system which the Church inherited from the Jews, preserved in the Bible, and pertinaciously defended against the heathen, it was still possible to maintain the unity of God while insisting on the deity of one who was distinct from God the Father.[1]

Is it, in short, possible, without logical absurdity, to conceive the relation of the Son to the Father in terms of the notion of derived equality? This is the question which was at stake in that whole mass of speculation and theorizing which culminated, though it by no means came to an end, in the definition by the Council of Nicaea of the truth that the Son is of the same substance as the Father, *homoousios tō Patri*. With the recognition of the full deity of the Son the doctrine of the Trinity was virtually established. It is true that the Church was for a time distracted by the Macedonian heresy, which denied the deity of the Holy Spirit; but the essential point of principle had been won at Nicaea. To quote Dr. Prestige again:

Down to the fourth century, the deity of the Holy Spirit

---

[1] Op. cit., p. 76.

came in for much less either of explicit assertion or of direct attack than that of the Son. Largely, this result was due to its raising no special problem; if the godhead was not unitary, it was as simple to conceive of three Persons as of two: hence the deity of Christ carried the weight of Trinitarian controversies without any necessity for extending the range of dispute, and as a matter of history, the settlement of the problems connected with the Father and the Son was found to lead to an immediate solution of the whole Trinitarian difficulty.[1]

We are, however, running ahead of our discussion. Later in this chapter I shall try to clarify the orthodox notion of derived equality within the Godhead; at the moment I wish to show how, in the various heretical alternatives which confronted the early Church, the two elements of this dual notion failed to hold together, so that we get in its place the two mutually opposed positions of equality without derivation on the one hand, and derivation without equality on the other.

There are two ways in which we can get a doctrine of equality without derivation and they are, surprisingly enough, as violently contrasted with each other as either of them is to the doctrine of derivation without equality. We may either hold with modalism that Father, Son and Holy Spirit are really identical, or with tritheism that they are entirely independent. In the former case we rule out derivation by reducing equality to identity; in the second case we rule it out by reducing equality to independence. Modalism or Sabellianism—the doctrine

[1] Ibid., p. 80.

that Father, Son and Holy Ghost are only three successive or alternating appearances assumed by the same individual and have no distinct reality or permanence—was a heresy with which the Church had seriously to grapple; though the text-book assertions, that the Sabellians referred to them as three *prosopa*, and that in the third century *prosōpon* meant either a mask or a character in a play, seem both to be unfounded.[1] Tritheism, on the other hand, was a position that no one who claimed to be Christian could very easily admit that he held, though the accusation was correspondingly damaging if it could be colourably levelled against one's opponents.

It is interesting to notice in passing that, largely owing to a difference in terminology, these two errors of modalism and tritheism are precisely the errors of which Greek and Latin theologians have tended to suspect each other. The formula upon which, after long discussion, the Orthodox East finally settled as expressing as adequately as possible the mystery of the divine Being was 'three *hypostases* in one *ousia*'; the formula ultimately accepted in the Catholic West was 'three *personae* in one *substantia*'. Now it is arguable that the opinions indicated by these two formulae, while equally orthodox, are not altogether identical. However, any difference that there is between them can be greatly exaggerated through a sheerly verbal confusion. On purely etymological grounds *hypostasis* and *substantia* ought to be precise equivalents, for each of them consists of the abstract noun from the verb 'to stand' preceded by an affix mean-

[1] Ibid., p. 113, 157f.

ing 'under'. The unwary Greek, hearing his Latin colleague professing belief in one *substantia* may easily interpret this as belief in one *hypostasis*; and, remembering
that he himself professes belief in three hypostases, he
may well mark down the Latin as a Sabellian. His
opinion of his colleague may be confirmed when he
notices that the word which the Latin is prepared to use
of each member of the Triad is *persona*, a term which in
one of its applications means an actor's mask or the
character denoted by it, and which would seem precisely to correspond to the meaning which, however
mistakenly, the word *prosōpon* was believed to have for
the Sabellians who, however mistakenly, were believed
to have used it. On the other hand, the over-hasty Latin,
when he hears the Greek asserting his belief in three
hypostases, may easily translate this as three *substantiae*,
and, remembering that he himself believes that there is
only one *substantia* of the Godhead, in so doing will
accuse the Greek of being a tritheist or at best an Arian.
The famous example of this misunderstanding and of its
elucidation is provided by the correspondence between
Dionysius of Rome and Dionysius of Alexandria in the
middle of the third century, in which the Alexandrian
had some difficulty in convincing his Roman namesake
that, in spite of his assertion of three divine *hypostases*,
he did not believe in more than one God. Similar suspi-
cions manifested themselves periodically in the West
down to the eleventh century or later, and they are
expressed by thinkers as eminent as St. Jerome and St.
Benedict of Aniane. The very greatest of the Latins,

however, including St. Augustine, St. Anselm and St. Thomas Aquinas, while recognizing a difference in theological outlook between East and West kept clear of this particular pitfall. Dr. Prestige has characterized the Eastern and Western doctrines in the phrases 'Three Objects' and 'Three Subjects' respectively;[1] if this formulation is adequate it shows a definite and important difference between Eastern and Western theology, but it is clear that neither is the first phrase more inclined to tritheism than the second, nor the second more inclined to modalism than the first.

Let us now see what happens when the aspect of derivation in the Holy Trinity is emphasized in such a way as to deny the genuine equality of the Persons. Here we are faced with that whole complex of theorizing which goes by the name of subordinationism, the view that Christ, even in his pre-incarnate condition, was definitely inferior to the Father. The most extreme form of subordinationism would, of course, deny Christ's pre-existence altogether. It would say either that Christ was never anything more than a man, though no doubt a very holy one (the view known as psilanthropism), or else that, although he was at some stage of his life elevated into a status of honorary sonship and deity, he was never, in the literal sense, *equal* to the Father (this is the view known as adoptionism). The most developed, as it was also the most menacing, form of this view was, however, provided by the Arian heresy in the early fourth century, and it will be instruc-

[1] Ibid., pp. 233–41.

tive to see how the labours of the great Athanasius and his orthodox colleagues culminated in its condemnation at Nicaea in A.D. 325 and its final rejection at Constantinople in 381.

The path along which Arianism hurled itself upon Christendom had been very largely prepared by the earlier Christian writers through their widespread habit of describing the preincarnate Christ as the *Logos* or 'Word' of God. In itself there was nothing in this term which was incompatible with the strictest orthodoxy; the first chapter of St. John's Gospel tells us that 'in the beginning was the Word, and the Word was with God, and the Word was God' and that 'the Word was made flesh and dwelt among us'. In the English translation the assertion that 'the Word was God' might seem to rule out any possibility of subordination; however the absence of the definite article before the word *Theos* in the Greek text makes it just possible to take the phrase as meaning merely that the Word was divine in some secondary and subordinate sense. And when the Christian Gospel was transferred from its original Jewish setting into the intellectual climate of the Greco-Roman world, the term *Logos* in its Christian usage inevitably attracted to itself the complicated and varied nuances that it had already acquired in a Gentile setting. Among these was the notion of the Logos as some kind of intermediary between the ultimate perfect divine being and the changing and differentiated world of which we are part. The gnostic heresies which had been the most dangerous opponents of Christianity in its earliest days had

made great play with the theory that the gulf between
the perfect changeless deity and the imperfect changing
world was bridged by an intricate series of intermediaries or *aeons*, which by their interwoven unions and
generations made it possible for the deity to be ultimately
responsible for the existence of the world without soiling
his hands too much in the process. The attempt to
bridge the gulf in this way was, in fact, doomed to
failure. As Prestige has remarked, the Gnostic Valen-
tinus, whose system contained no less than thirty aeons,

> strangely ignored the fact that, though every declension
> from perfect goodness and power was thus reduced to a
> comparatively narrow interval, yet in the aggregate the
> chasm between God and the existing world of sense re-
> mains the same. Thirty successive gaps, though small, and
> arranged on a graduated scale, can assist the mind no more
> readily than one immense gap to comprehend the inter-
> action of two such diverse factors as infinite spirit and
> sensuous existence.[1]

I suggested in the last chapter that the notion of intermediaries between God and creatures is a thoroughly
pagan notion. We may also note that the picture of
God and creatures as separated by a gulf, gap or chasm
which needs to be bridged is a thoroughly incoherent
picture. For since everything that exists is either God or
creatures, what is there out of which a bridge between
God and creatures could be made? Nevertheless,
gnosticism died hard, and even when it was realized that
a crowd of intermediaries could not really *diminish* the

[1] *Fathers and Heretics*, p. 62.

gap, the notion persisted that one intermediary could in some way *bridge* it. Logically if not altogether chronologically, this step was taken, with the result that some types of Logos-doctrine can be fairly described as a form of gnosticism in which there is only one aeon. Superficially there might seem to be Biblical support for such a view, but only superficially. The Old Testament habitually describes creation as resulting from a word or utterance of God. 'God said, Let there be light, and there was light. . . . God said, Let the earth bring forth the living creature after its kind, cattle and creeping thing and beast of the earth after its kind; and it was so.'[1] 'By the word of the Lord were the heavens made; and all the host of them by the breath of his mouth.'[2] We need, however, only to look at the whole context of passages such as these in order to see that the word by which God is here alleged to create is not an emanation of the divine substance but a sheer utterance of the divine will. The God of the Bible shows his power, not by being able to eject from himself an intermediary which is his agent in the work of creation, but by being able to create without any intermediary at all. Only in the later apocryphal books of the Old Testament do we find something approaching the view of the Logos as an intermediary, in the mysterious figure of the divine Wisdom, possessed (or, as the better known reading said, *created*) by God in the beginning of his way, and with him as a master-workman when he created the heavens

---

[1] Gen. i: 3, 24.
[2] Psalm xxxiii: 6.

and the earth.[1] it was, however, by appealing to such passages as these that some case could be made out for the position that the Logos, while vastly superior to everything else except God the Father, was only to be described as God in a secondary or subordinate sense; and this was accentuated when a distinction was made between the immanence of the Logos in the Father from all eternity and the 'expression' or utterance of Logos in creation, with the implication that it was only in creation that the Logos achieved full personal status and distinct existence. The way was thus paved for the heresy of Arius at the beginning of the fourth century, with his teaching that the Word or Son, while he was superior to all other creatures and was the Father's agent in their creation, was nevertheless a creature himself when all was said and done, and with the further consequence that, although the Son did not come into being at a moment of time, since time itself came into being with the world, yet there was, if not time, at least something to which temporal language can be applied, 'when he was not'.

It has often been remarked that one of Arius's aims, whether conscious or not, was to make Christianity easy for the multitudes of half-converted heathen who were flooding into the Church as a result of the toleration, and later the adoption, of the Christian Church by the emperor Constantine. It is illuminating to see how this was so. Arius's attribution to the Son of what Christian orthodoxy could only characterize as a fictitious or

[1] Prov. viii: 22f. Cf. Wisd. ix: 9.

bogus deity was not the consequence of a desire to deprive the Son of divine honour; far from it. He was anxious to make it easy for people to adore the Son with all the accompaniments of divine worship. His unexpunged paganism was shown by the fact that he firmly believed that it was possible to do this while holding that the Son was God only in a secondary sense. To do this came only too naturally to those who had recently been accustomed to render a religious cultus to Olympian heroes, tutelary spirits and recently deceased, or even still living, emperors. But to those who had only just emerged from the menacing shadow of persecution and who were firmly rooted in the Biblical tradition, with its roots in Palestinian Judaism, this was nothing less than apostasy. Thus the fundamental pagan error of the Arians was not that they refused to give divine honour to Christ, but that they were perfectly willing to give him divine honour while holding that he was not God in the strict monotheistic sense. That this position was indeed fundamentally pagan will be realized when we recall that, in the days of persecution, the unforgivable offence of Christians was not that they adored the Father and the Son and the Holy Spirit, but that they refused to adore the Emperor or anyone else.

It was, then, the basic contention of the Arians that the Son could not derive his being from the Father without being inferior to him. This is what underlay the various words—*homoiousios, homoios, anomoios*—which the different brands of Arians and semi-Arians proposed as alternatives to the Athanasian *homoousios*. The Son might be of similar substance to the Father, or simply similar to the Father, or flatly unlike the Father; what he could not be was of the same substance as the Father. A son is younger than his father and inferior to him; that is all there is to be said.

What had therefore to be replied to the Arians was that the Father and the Son were of exactly the same kind of stuff, namely deity; this was what was primarily implied by the word *homoousios* on the lips of Athanasius and his followers. How this was possible without the Father and the Son being either, on the one hand, the same Person or, on the other hand, two distinct Gods was a matter that would have to be looked into; it was not the immediate point at issue. The *ousia* which, according to the *homoousios* formula, was the same in Father and Son was not the individualized substance, the *prōtē ousia* of the philosophers, which is different in two subjects even if they are of the same species; *homoousios* in that sense would imply Sabellianism, though the view that the term had been rejected in 268 by the Synod of Antioch on that ground has been alleged to rest upon a misunderstanding.[1] It was the *deutera ousia*, the specific essence, not different but identical in two individuals of the same species, that the *homoousios* affirmed to be the same in the Father and the Son; and in this sense *homoousios* is fully coherent with the trinitarian formula of the Greeks, which declares that the three divine *hypostaseis* are united in one *ousia*.

Coherent, yes, but hardly synonymous, for if we left

---

[1] Cf. Prestige, *God in Patristic Thought*, p. 202f.

the matter here the *homoousios* doctrine would be equally
compatible with ditheism or tritheism. Peter, James and
John are individually man and are collectively three
men. The Father, the Son and the Holy Spirit are individually God; are they then collectively three Gods?
'The Father is God, the Son is God, and the Holy Ghost
is God', declares *Quicunque vult*; but if *homoousios* means
what we have just said, can we go on with it to assert
'And yet there are not three Gods, but one God'?
Athanasius certainly realized that if *homoousios* primarily
referred to specific essence, it also included much more;
he was no more a Sabellian than he was an Arian. But
it was the great work of the three Cappadocian Fathers,
Basil the Great, his brother Gregory of Nyssa and their
friend Gregory of Nazianzum, to bring out the full meaning of *homoousios*. At the moment we shall take up the
story from an earlier point.

2. FROM HOMOOUSIOS TO PERICHORESIS

When the Arians insisted that a son is always younger
than his father, the orthodox reply was that this juniority
and inferiority are not essential to sonship as such; they
are incidental to sonship as it is manifested in a world of
genesis and *phthora*, of coming-to-be and passing-away.
Even in this world of change and decay, people are frequently junior and inferior to others without being their
sons; the essence of sonship is not juniority or inferiority,
but derivation. Indeed, once we abstract from it the accidental characteristics of temporal development, we see

that even on earth sonship implies equality rather than inferiority. When a son has grown up and his father has died, he can, simply in virtue of his sonship, step into his father's shoes and assume the property, status and responsibilities which his father had formerly exercised. To take a modern instance, the eldest son of the Marquess of X, on his father's demise, becomes himself the Marquess of X precisely because he is his father's son; the fact that his peerage has been acquired by inheritance from his father is not made a reason for degrading him to the level of an earl or a viscount. It was the realization that begetting implies equality, that led the Church ultimately to make the sharpest of distinctions between the notions of begetting or generation on the one hand and making or creation on the other. The story of this is a fascinating one and it forms one of the major themes of Prestige's *God in Patristic Thought*. The matter was complicated by the remarkable fact that the words for 'begotten' and for 'made' in Greek are identical in sound and almost identical in spelling. 'Begotten' is *gennētos*, and 'made' is *genētos*, and the Christian doctrines of creation and of Christ depend upon keeping their meanings unconfused. For 'begotten', as we have seen, implies equality, while 'made' implies inferiority. If we describe the world as begotten, instead of as made, we shall fall into some form of pantheism; if, on the other hand, we describe the Logos as made, instead of as begotten, we shall reduce him to the level of a creature. *Genētos* not *gennētos* for the world; *gennētos* not *genētos* for the Logos—this is the pattern of Christian orthodoxy, though the Church was long in achieving a clear realization how necessary was this distinction of words for the preservation of the faith. But she realized it clearly in the end, and it lies behind the great assertions of *Quicunque vult.* 'The Father is made from none, neither created nor begotten. The Son is from the Father alone, not made, nor created, but begotten. The Holy Ghost is from the Father and the Son, not made, nor created, nor begotten, but proceeding.'

The Son, then, is equal to the Father, but equal with a derived equality; begotten from the Father, but begotten with an eternal generation. Light from Light, true God from true God, in the words of the Nicene Creed; begotten from his Father before all worlds. The generation of the Son is fully in line with *homoousios*, as that had come to be understood through the Arian controversy. But, to return to our previous point, does this distinction between Father and Son altogether rule out the danger of ditheism or tritheism?

That the danger was by no means fictitious is shown in the last three chapters of Dr. Prestige's great book, and in order to see how the Church finally evaded it I shall follow the main lines of his exposition. It is perhaps natural that the Cappadocian Fathers, with their vigorous defence of Nicene orthodoxy, should sometimes have been accused of virtual tritheism; the accusation is, however, unjust. They make it quite plain that the way in which the three Persons participate in Godhead is quite different from the way in which a number of human beings participate in manhood.

The differences that distinguish different human beings are manifold; but the differences that distinguish the divine Persons consist simply in the 'idiotetes' expressed in the names of Fatherhood, Sonship, and Sanctification. . . . The whole unvaried common substance, being incomposite, is identical with the whole unvaried being of each Person; there is no question of accidents attaching to it; the entire substance of the Son is the same as the entire substance of the Father; the individuality is only the manner in which the identical substance is objectively presented in each several person.[1]

There is in fact nothing that differentiates the three Persons except their mutual interordination, expressed by the three particularities of *agennēsia*, *gennēsis* and *ekpempsis*: ingeneration, generation and promission.[2] This is substantially the same point that will later on be made in the West by St. Thomas Aquinas, when he insists that the distinctive denominations of the three Persons denote pure relations, although relations that are real and intrinsic to the Godhead, and that the processions in virtue of which the three Persons are distinct are wholly internal processions.

Anything that proceeds by a procession which is *ad extra* must be diverse from that from which it proceeds. But that which proceeds by an intelligible process *ad intra* need not be diverse; indeed, the more perfectly it proceeds the more it is one with that from which it proceeds.[3]

The matter was clinched when the Cappadocians applied to the three divine Persons the phrase *tropos*

[1] Op. cit., p. 243.   [2] Ibid., p. 245.   [3] *S. Theol.*, I, xxvii, 1 *ad* 2.

hyparxeōs or 'mode of existence'. By this they meant that the whole Godhead in its concrete totality was instantiated in each of the persons, paternally in the Father, filially in the Son, and pneumatically in the Spirit.

> The term mode of hyparxis [writes Prestige] was applied, from the end of the fourth century, to the particularities that distinguish the divine Persons, in order to express the belief that in those Persons or hypostaseis one and the same divine being is presented in distinct objective and permanent expressions, though with no variation in divine content.[1]

The whole Godhead, not as a logical universal but as a concrete existent, possessed wholly by each Person in the way appropriate to each; this was the doctrine of the Cappadocians. It had a remarkable and important result, which is luminously stated in the following paragraph from Prestige's work:

> One salutary consequence followed from the fact that the basis of thought was now laid in the triplicity of objective presentation rather than the unity of essential being. It meant the end of subordinationism. There was no longer any question but that the Son and the Holy Spirit are indeed equal to the Father as touching divinity, since each is a presentation of an identical divine being. The history of Arius had indicated that subordinationism leads either to unitarianism or to polytheism, or to a mixture of the two. The only sense in which the doctrine could survive in Catholic theology was in strict and sole relation to the doctrine of arche. According to this doctrine, the Father's mode of hyparxis involves a logical, though of course not

[1] Op. cit., p. 248.

a temporal, priority, in that the two derivative modes of hyparxis, those of the Son and of the Holy Spirit, depend on it for their source. But such priority involves no superiority. The doctrine of the Trinity, as formulated by the Cappadocians, may be summed up in the phrase that God is one object *in* himself and three objects *to* himself. Further than that illuminating paradox it is difficult to see that human thought can go. It secures both the unity and the trinity.[1]

'Both the unity and the trinity'—this is the essential point. We might be tempted to think that the doctrine of the *tropoi hyparxeōs*, with its insistence upon the objective threefoldness of presentation, might somewhat minimize the unity of the Godhead and give colour to the accusation that the Cappadocians were tritheists. The opposite is the case. For the particularities of ingeneration, generation and promission are not merely distinguishing features of the three Persons; they are their only distinguishing features. (As a Thomist would say, the three Persons differ from each other in nothing but the processions, and in the relations and notions that arise from the processions.) 'The implication of this fact', writes Prestige, 'is that the unity of God, though sometimes in the background, continued to be held with great tenacity.'[2] We might well think that, so far at least as the Christian East was concerned, trinitarian theology had reached its final phase and that nothing remained to be added. There was, however, a further step to be taken, and it was the result of a peculiar withdrawal on the

[1] Ibid., p. 249.   [2] Ibid., p. 256.

part of certain theologians from the concrete robustness of the Cappadocians into the realm of logical discourse.

This movement, which was largely due to a tendency to assimilate the concepts of trinitarian theology to those of Christology, reaches a clear expression in the writings of two sixth-century theologians, Leontius of Byzantium and Leontius of Jerusalem, and it even affected their far greater junior Maximus the Confessor. The orthodox doctrine of the Incarnation, as established at the Council of Chalcedon in the year 451, is that in Christ two whole and perfect natures, a divine and a human, coinhere, without confusion or separation, in the one divine Person of God the Son. Two natures in one Person, two *physeis* in one *hypostasis*, is the truth about Christ. In Aristotelian philosophy, however, *physis* and *ousia* are practically identical, as are *natura* and *essentia* in scholastic Latin. What can therefore be more tempting than to place alongside the Christological formula 'Two *physeis* in one *hypostasis*' the trinitarian formula 'Three *hypostaseis* in one *physis*', and to place alongside the trinitarian formula 'Three *hypostaseis* in one *ousia*' the Christological formula 'Two *ousiai* in one *hypostasis*'? Nothing could appear to be less objectionable or more edifying; and yet the verbal similarities of the formulae bring back again that very instability and ambiguity in the meaning of *ousia* from which the Cappadocians seemed to have rescued it. For, unless we are to fall into the Nestorian heresy of dividing Christ into two individuals, the word *ousia*, now used as identical with *physis*, cannot have the fully concrete sense of the philosophers' *prōtē ousia*; it must, like *physis* itself, indicate the specific nature rather than the individual existence, since what the Logos united to himself in becoming incarnate was manhood, not a man. If now we take this sense of *ousia* into the trinitarian formula, the plain implication will be that the three Persons are three individual members of a species 'God', and the safeguards which the Cappadocians erected against tritheism will have vanished. As Prestige remarks, when Leontius of Jerusalem is expounding the Incarnation he is clear and satisfactory.

> But when he turns to the Trinity, and applies a form of definition which attaches the whole concrete element in the conception to the hypostasis, treating the physis as concrete solely in its dependence on the hypostasis, his theory fails to exclude tritheism. The only concrete residua are the hypostaseis, and they are three. . . . The whole mischief lay in his deplorable assimilation of *ousia* to *physis*, which made of it, not perhaps a secondary ousia (which would have involved a definite form of tritheism, with three Gods all made of a common stuff), but an abstract analysis, which might or might not imply identity, as opposed to similarity, of substance.[1]

We need not pursue this point any further; the issue is sufficiently plain. It is, however, interesting to observe that Prestige sees this reversal of tradition in the sixth and seventh centuries as directly due to the triumph of the Council of Chalcedon, and suggests that Chalcedon saved Christology from heresy at the cost of making theology abstract where it had previously been concrete.

[1] Ibid., p. 275.

Negatively, it was a crowning mercy: it suppressed psychology, to the avoidance of untold heresy, though also to the complete postponement of positive Christological advance. Official Christology remained negative and abstract, and for that reason abstraction became a necessity of theological thought.[1]

I am not sure that I agree with this somewhat lukewarm approbation of Chalcedon, or with the implied unfavourable judgment upon abstract thought. The use of abstraction is, after all, one of the ways in which we think about concrete realities. What is lamentable, however, is to think about concrete realities as if they themselves were abstractions, and it is this, as Prestige shows, that seems to have happened in the trinitarian theology of the sixth and seventh centuries. It was the very success of Chalcedon in the Christological realm—and that was, after all, its main job—that led to an uncritical and formalistic extension of its concepts to the trinitarian realm, in which they were not altogether appropriate. The situation was saved, as Prestige goes on to show, by an anonymous thinker who, in fact, did much more than save the situation; and who gave trinitarian theology an organic completeness which even the Cappadocians had failed to give it, by his introduction of the notion of *perichōrēsis* or 'coinherence'.

In Maximus the Confessor the term *perichōrēsis* is used to denote the reciprocity that holds between the two natures of Christ in virtue of their inherence in the one divine Person of the Son. But the anonymous theologian

[1] Ibid., p. 280.

whose works are appended to those of St. Cyril of Alexandria, transferred it from a Christological to a trinitarian setting. Unlike the parallel transference of *physis* by the Leontii, the result was all to the good; and the term acquired a more, instead of a less, concrete connotation through the change of context. It now described the complete mutual interpenetration and embracement of the three divine Persons through the possession by each, in its own proper way, of the totality of the divine Substance. Sabellianism, Arianism and tritheism are equally excluded, and with the incorporation of the greater part of pseudo-Cyril into the treatise *De Fide Orthodoxa* by St. John of Damascus in the eighth century, the notion of *perichōrēsis* brought Greek trinitarian theology to its final state, in which the doctrine of derived equality is at last safe from both modalism and tritheism on the one side and from subordinationism on the other.

It only remains to add, before we turn to the West, that long before this stage had been reached, the Logos-doctrine had to all intents and purposes been discarded. Once it was made plain at Nicaea that the Logos was of the same stuff as the Father, any possibility of making the Logos an intermediary between God and the world was destroyed. In the words of Dr. Leonard Hodgson:

> Harnack was surely right in holding that the triumph of Athanasius at Nicaea marked the final failure of the attempt to expound the relation of the Second to the First Person in the godhead by means of the idea of the Logos-Creator. The assertion of the full godhead of the Son, 'of one sub-

stance with the Father', whether or no he might continue to be called Logos or Verbum, meant that he no longer occupied an intermediary position between Creator and created. The Jewish belief in direct creation by the will of a personal God broke free from its uneasy entanglement with an alien and inconsistent metaphysic.[1]

3. THE WESTERN DEVELOPMENT

In its attitude to the Trinity, as in so many other questions, Western theology since the fifth century has been dominated by the colossal figure of St. Augustine of Hippo, and it is notable that the main features of his teaching reappear in figures as diverse as the thirteenth-century scholastic St. Thomas Aquinas and the sixteenth-century reformer John Calvin.[2] In his treatise on the Trinity the great African father supplements the primarily metaphysical approach of the Greek theologians to the mystery of the divine Being with analogies derived from the created realm. Perhaps his best known analogy is that in which, starting from the Johannine truth that God is Love, he compares the Persons of the Trinity with the lover, the beloved and the love that unites the two—*amans, et quod amatur, et amor.*[3] Far more important, however, is his use of a psychological analogy, in which he sees the three Persons as personally existent analogues of the basic operations of the human mind. This analogy appears in more than one form. The

[1] *The Doctrine of the Trinity*, p. 122.
[2] Cf. L. Hodgson, *The Doctrine of the Trinity*, ch. vi.
[3] *De Trinitate*, viii, 14.

earlier statement of it sees the Father as the divine Mind, and the Son and the Spirit as his hypostatized operations of Knowledge and Love; the triad consists of *mens, notitia, amor,*[1] and there is an obvious disparity between the first member and the other two. The second statement sees all three Persons as hypostatized operations of the divine Mind which is the One God; and the triad consists of *memoria, intelligentia, voluntas*; memory, intelligence and will.[2] It is, incidentally, important to observe that the object of these three operations is taken as being the mind itself, not any external object. This is especially significant in the case of memory. The view of the soul as having three primary modes of operation, rather than the mere dyad of intelligence and will, is not uncommon in Christian thought; it makes an impressive appearance in the sixteenth century in St. John of the Cross, who sees the three operations of intellect, memory and will as purged respectively by the three theological virtues of faith, hope and charity.[3] Almost invariably, however, as in the case just cited, memory is placed after intellect and indeed is seen as akin to it; so that in fact the triadic and dyadic psychologies differ less than might appear at first sight. In St. Augustine's trinitarian use, on the other hand, memory comes first, as corresponding to God the Father, and we can see why this is when we realize that the object of each of the operations is the mind itself; the triad is *memoria sui, intelligentia sui, voluntas sui.* God's memory of himself, therefore, is not a reflexive operation subsequent upon the formation of an

---

[1] Ibid., ix.   [2] Ibid., x.   [3] Cf. *Ascent of Mount Carmel,* II, vi *et passim.*

intelligible object; it is, as it were, the self-recollection or self-possession which precedes the evocation of any intellectual or voluntary act.[1] It is interesting to notice that St. Augustine himself considers this second form of the triad as the more helpful for his purpose; it is *evidentior trinitas.*[2] St. Thomas agrees with him.[3]

We may discount at the start the obvious objection that the use of this psychological analogy is simply equivalent to modalism, that it reduces the three Persons to three operations of one Substantial mind. St. Augustine, like St. Thomas after him, is clear where the analogy ceases to apply and where it needs to be supplemented. It is noticeable that, although St. Thomas considers St. Augustine's psychological analogy as highly useful for the interpretation of the doctrine of the Trinity, he does not identify it with a dogmatic statement of the doctrine itself.[4] Through article after article he expounds the doctrine in terms of the classical patristic notions of *hypostasis, persona, substantia, paternity, filiation, procession* and

[1] Cf. A. Gardeil, *La Structure de l'Ame et l'Expérience Mystique*, I, p. 21f.

[2] *De Trin.*, xv, 5.   [3] *S. Theol.*, I, xciii, 7 ad 2.

[4] Professor V. Lossky remarks that in Eastern orthodox theology 'it is never said, for example, that the Son proceeds after the manner of intelligence and the Holy Spirit after the manner of will. The Spirit is never assimilated to the love of the Father and the Son. The trinitarian psychologism of St. Augustine is seen rather as an analogical image than as a positive theology expressing the relations of the Persons' (*Théologie Mystique de l'Église d'Orient*, p. 78 shortly to be published in an English translation by Messrs. James Clarke & Co. Ltd., and here quoted by permission). Contrary to what is commonly supposed, I think St. Thomas would have agreed with the judgment expressed in the last sentence.

the rest, with hardly a mention of intelligence or will; and although, for example, he finds it illuminating to think of the procession of the Word from the Father as analogous to the formation of a concept by the intellect, he is explicit that the primary name of the procession of the Word is not intellection but generation.[1] We may note again that St. Thomas does not hold that the Son and the Spirit are simply hypostatized operations, but that they exist in virtue of the exercise of those operations in the Godhead. The Son is not called Intelligence, but Word and Image; the Spirit is not called Will, but Love and Gift.[2] It has sometimes been suggested that, under the influence of St. Augustine, Western theology has entirely lost the notion of the *monarchia* of the Father and has substituted for it the notion of the metaphysical antecedence of the divine Essence; that it thinks of God not in terms of the Father generating the Son from all eternity and of the Father and the Son promitting the Spirit, but in terms of the one divine substance differentiating itself by an interior self-triplication. Now it is, of course, possible to consider the triune God from either aspect, and it is in fact fruitful to do so. But one need only glance at the headings of the articles in St. Thomas's treatise on the Trinity in the *Pars Prima* to see how far he is from forgetting the inherent ordination of the Persons to one another. He is indeed determined to rule out any subordination of the Arian type, but the priority of the Father is the starting point of his exposition. And a passage like the following makes it emphatically clear

[1] *S. Theol.*, I, xxvii, 2.   [2] Ibid., I, xxxiv–xxxviii.

how determined the Angelic Doctor is to maintain both
the fundamental relatedness of the Persons and also the
complete possession by each of the totality of the Godhead:

> Distinction within God (*in divinis*) is made only by rela-
> tions of origin. . . . But a relation in God is not like an
> accident inhering in a subject; it is the divine essence itself;
> therefore it is subsistent, as the divine essence subsists.
> Therefore, as deity is God, so divine paternity is God the
> Father, who is a divine Person. A divine Person therefore
> means a relation as subsisting. And this means a relation by
> the manner of a substance which is a hypostasis subsisting
> in the divine nature; although what subsists in the divine
> nature is the divine nature itself.

It is no part of my present purpose to give a full exposition of the teaching of St. Thomas concerning the
Holy Trinity. All that I want to make plain is that, in
spite of the difference of outlook which has been already
mentioned, and of the popularity of the celebrated
psychological analogy of St. Augustine, the West no
less than the East has held to the doctrine of derived
equality without diverging into either modalism or
tritheism. The notion of *perichōrēsis* in which the East
came to rest finds its counterpart in the Western doctrine of subsistent relations, a doctrine which was in fact
developed by St. Augustine and which in his own discussion holds an anterior place to the psychological
analogy, though it is much more briefly expounded.

In discussing this doctrine as it is understood by St.

Augustine and St. Thomas, it is more than usually important to remember that when terms and concepts from some other realm are introduced into the realm of theology, they are to be understood not univocally but analogically. There must be some common element, some *perfectio significata*, in common between their non-theological and their theological use, or there would be no point in introducing them into theology at all; but the shade of meaning, the *modus significandi*, which they have in theology is to be gathered not from their original but from their theological usage. Now in Aristotelian logic, relation is one of the ten categories or 'predicaments', one of the 'forms of incomplex signification', which between them comprehend the various ways in which a predicate can be attributed to a subject. Of these categories the first is that of substance, and all the other nine, including that of relation, are 'accidental'; that is to say, they could, at least in thought, be removed without the destruction of the subject. It was the brilliant idea of St. Augustine, that, if he removed relation from the sub-class of accidents and placed it in that which had hitherto been occupied exclusively by substance, he would have a fruitful analogy for the Persons of the Trinity. Nothing, he tells us, is spoken of God accidentally, but according to substance or relation.[1] It will thus be possible to maintain that the three Persons are identical as regards their substance or *ousia*, while really distinct from each other through the different relations in which they stand to it. Everything that belongs to one

[1] *De Trinitate*, v, 6.

Person belongs to the other two—*all* are omnipotent, *all* are omniscient, *all* are wise, true, good and so on. All that differentiates them is their relations: paternity in the Father, filiality in the Son, procession in the Spirit. The whole Godhead is possessed paternally in the Father, filially in the Son, and with whatever adverb is proper to the third Person (for here the available vocabulary breaks down) in the Spirit. However different in its dress, this formulation is thoroughly coherent with that of the earlier Fathers in the East, for example, with the Cappadocian insistence that nothing distinguishes the three Persons except their mutual interordination, expressed by the three particularities of *agennēsia*, *gennēsis* and *ekpempsis* respectively.[1] The only difference is that, whereas the Easterns tended to think primarily in terms of the relations of the persons to one another, the West, with Augustine, tended to think of the different relations of the Persons to the one Godhead or divine substance. The Western outlook is, however, already anticipated by the Cappadocian concept of the *tropoi hyparxeōs*. Perhaps the most comprehensive way of stating the matter would be to say that the relations of the three Persons to the one divine essence are themselves expressed in terms of their relations to one another—paternity, filiation, spiration—or that the different ways in which each of the Persons is God arise solely from the processions, from the generation of the Son and the spiration of the Holy Ghost. In this way it should be possible to allay the suspicion under which both the Cappadocian

[1] Cf. p. 63 *supra.*

and the Augustinian triadology have sometimes fallen, that they view the divine essence as something subsisting anteriorly to the three Persons. Godhead can exist only paternally, filially or by spiration; nowhere is it to be found but in the Father, the Son and the Holy Ghost.

It may be added that in St. Thomas we find the matter clinched by a further distinction, that between the relations and the notions. The relations hold in each case *between* the Persons, whereas the notions are the distinguishing particularities *in* the Persons consequent upon the relations. And all these are ultimately based upon the processions. There are in God two processions, namely the *generation* of the Son and the *double procession* of the Spirit (for St. Thomas, of course, holds with all the later Westerns that the Spirit proceeds not from the Father alone, but from the Father and the Son). There are four relations: *paternity*, of the Father to the Son; *filiation*, of the Son to the Father; *spiration*, of the Father and the Son, as one principle, to the Spirit; and *procession*, of the Spirit to the Father and the Son. And there are five notions or 'proper ideas for knowing a divine Person': *unbegottenness* (innascibilitas) and *paternity* for the Father; *filiation* for the Son; *common spiration* for the Father and also for the Son; and *procession* for the Spirit. And the Angelic Doctor laments the verbal duplication which is necessary as a result of the paucity of words for use in connection with the Spirit.[1]

I shall refer again to this doctrine of subsistent relations in connection with the Incarnation.[2] Here I need

---

[1] *S. Theol.*, I, xxvii; xxviii, 4; xxxii, 3.   [2] Cf. p. 110 *infra*.

only emphasize that the Unity in Trinity, which in the East is expressed by the coinherence of the Persons in each other, is expressed in the West by the real identity of the divine nature with the Persons, each of whom possesses it in its totality after his own manner. To describe such a view as 'abstract' is surely inadmissible, unless we are to describe the divine nature itself as abstract. It is in fact the doctrine of the divine Persons as subsistent relations, as St. Augustine and St. Thomas understand it, which makes it plain that the divine nature is not just a logical universal but is the supreme self-existent Reality upon whose loving and creative will the existence of everything other than himself depends.

III

UNCONFUSED UNION
THE DOCTRINE OF THE INCARNATION

I. CHALCEDONIAN ORTHODOXY AND THE ALTERNATIVES

It was the primary concern of the Council of Nicaea to make it plain beyond all possibility of misunderstanding that Jesus of Nazareth, while personally distinct from the Father, is God in the fullest sense of the word. God by derivation, indeed; God in the possession of communicated deity; but for this very reason equal to the Father and not inferior to him, equal with a derived equality. Had the Church been prepared to make the least concession to Arianism, all would have been plain sailing for the human mind; once admit the Son to be a creature however different from all other creatures and however highly exalted above them, and no special problem about his relation to the Father remains. He may be dignified with the title of God in some purely honorary and honorific sense; but however much this may scandalize the moral conscience of a strict monotheist, it will at least raise no difficulties for his intellect. The Father will remain alone transcendent, in the tremendous isolation of his incommunicable deity; he and none but he will be, literally and unfiguratively, God. What the Church came plainly to recognize, as the result of the labours of St. Athanasius and his friends, was that, small as were the demands that such a view made upon the human intellect, it was totally inadequate as an interpretation either of the position which Jesus had assumed for himself in his earthly ministry or of the experience of him which Christians had enjoyed through their life as members of his body. God from God, Light from Light, true God from true God, consubstantial with the Father; it was the Church's determination to maintain this doctrine of derived equality without deviating into either modalism or tritheism, that led her on the long intellectual pilgrimage whose goal was the full understanding of that mutual interpenetration of the three divine Persons, through their union in the one divine Essence, which is denoted by the word *perichōrēsis*. Only when the divinity of the Son had been firmly established could the Church give her full attention to the fact that the Son, being God, had become man; but once it was firmly established it was inevitable that she should do so.

The first chapter of St. John's Gospel tells us quite simply that 'the Word became flesh and dwelt among us'. Two points need to be noticed. The first is that in Hebrew idiom flesh (or flesh and blood) means not just the material part of a man in contrast with his soul or spirit, but human nature as a whole. The second is that St. John does not say that the Word united flesh to himself, but that he *became* flesh (*sarx egeneto*). St. Athanasius was fundamentally clear on this point. In

general, however, he is quite content to think of the Incarnation as taking place through the union of human
flesh or a human body to the divine Word. 'He took
upon him our flesh, as Aaron did his robe, and assumed
a body like ours, having Mary for the Mother of his
Body.'[1] 'The Word of God, out of his great love for
man, at the will of the Father, invests himself with our
mortal flesh.'[2] 'He, the mighty one, the artificer of all,
himself prepared this body in the Virgin as a temple for
himself and took it for his very own, as the instrument
through which he was known and in which he dwelt.'[3]
This concept of the incarnate Lord as consisting of *Logos*
plus *sarx*, Word plus flesh or body, was sufficient so long
as it was not taken too literally or analysed too minutely,
especially as it is abundantly clear that St. Athanasius
never intended, in using it, to imply that Christ was
devoid of a human mentality. The matter became very
different when his friend Apollinarius, who had spent
most of his life in an indefatigable defence of the
homoousios, began in his old age to interpret the Athanasian formulation in the most literal way. Some of the
accusations which were brought against him by his great
opponents the Cappadocian Fathers are now generally
dismissed as resting on a misunderstanding of his words;
in particular he seems never to have taught that, when
Christ was born of Mary, the Logos brought into the
world with him a pre-existent human nature from
heaven.[4] On the main point of his teaching, however,

[1] II *c. Arianos* 7.　　[2] II *c. Arianos* 65.　　[3] *De Incarn.* 8.
[4] Cf. C. E. Raven, *Apollinarianism*, pp. 185f, 212f.

Apollinarius's condemnation stands unreversed. He asserted that the place which in human beings in general is taken by a human mind or *nous* was occupied in Christ by the divine Logos, and he defended this theory on two grounds. The first was that it excluded any possibility of duplicating the personality of Christ; there were not two rational principles in the Saviour, namely the divine Logos and a human *nous*, but the one divine Logos and nothing else. The second ground of defence was a peculiarly perverse one. Apollinarius alleged quite correctly that the seat of human sinfulness is not in the flesh but in the mind. We are sinners not, as the Manichaeans held, because we have material bodies and matter is fundamentally gross and evil—matter is in fact good, because it is created by God and is subject to his control. We are sinners because we have misused our free will, and free will is a function of the mind. Apollinarius drew, however, from this undoubted truth the quite false conclusion that, since Christ was sinless, he must be devoid of a human mind altogether, the place of a human mind being taken by the divine Logos, who, as the intellectual principle of the Godhead, was eminently fitted to exercise the functions of mentality. Prestige has pointed out the amazing fact that, whether or not Apollinarius rethought for himself this doctrine of a mindless humanity in Christ, it appears to have been first propounded by certain Arians or even by Arius himself, though at the time it attracted little attention. 'The battle with Arianism had been fought on the question whether the Saviour were truly God; if he were not that, it made little odds

that an abbreviated deity should be united to a trun-
cated humanity.'[1] By the latter part of the fourth century, however, such teaching could hardly be over-
looked, and this for two reasons. First, while the
Apollinarian doctrine preserved the unity of Christ, it
did it at the expense of making him something less than
fully man. Secondly and more specifically, the fact that
the seat of human sin is the mind made it necessary, not
that the Redeemer should be devoid of a human mind
but, on the contrary, that he should possess a human
mind which was sinless. It was precisely the element in
us which is most perverted that it was most necessary
for the Logos to assume if, in the Incarnation, the human
race was to be re-created. In the pungent phrase of
Gregory Nazianzen, 'not assumed is not healed'.[2] Apollinarianism was condemned at the Council of Constantinople in the year 381; but the question which Apollinarius had raised was not to be easily answered. It was
the question whether the completeness and the distinc-
ness of the humanity and the divinity in Christ could be
preserved without detriment to his unity and their
union. Apollinarius had provided for the unity of
Christ and for the union between his humanity and his
divinity, but only at the expense of mutilating the
humanity and replacing its dominant constituent by
divinity. Can there be in Christ an unconfused union of
Godhead and manhood? This is the question which was
to exercise the minds of theologians and throw the life
of the Church into turmoil from Constantinople to

[1] *Fathers and Heretics*, p. 235.   [2] *Ep.* ci. 7.

Chalcedon seventy years later; and the unreconciled remnants of the dispute remain to this day in the still vigorous though diminished monophysite churches and the pathetic fragment which is all that is left of the once great Nestorian communion. It is the question which we shall consider in this chapter.

It is sometimes suggested that the great Christological controversies of the fourth and fifth centuries were nothing but intellectual rationalizations of two great political rivalries, the academic rivalry between the two great theological schools of Alexandria and Antoich, and the ecclesiastical rivalry between the ancient and learned patriarchate of Alexandria and the imperially favoured parvenu patriarchate of Constantinople. It is admittedly impossible to read the history of the period without becoming painfully impressed by the fact that many passions entered into the struggle besides the disinterested passion for the purity of the Gospel. Nevertheless, it would be totally untrue to suppose that the theological issues involved were either spurious or unimportant. What the orthodox Fathers were striving to do, and what was ultimately achieved at Chalcedon, was to preserve the doctrine of unconfused union of Godhead and manhood in Christ against tendencies which strove, on the one side, to unite the two terms at the cost of confusing them with each other and, on the other side, to keep them distinct at the cost of separating them. To us who look back upon Chalcedon after fifteen hundred years the notion of unconfused union in Christ may not seem to offer any special difficulty; that this is

so is a sign of the triumph of Chalcedon in our theological thought. In the fifth century it was a notion that
could only be achieved at the cost of bitter controversy
and schism.

The contrast between the outlooks of the schools of
Alexandria and Antioch has often been diagnosed as the
contrast between emphasis upon the divine and upon
the human; it can however equally well be characterized
as the contrast between unitary and pluralistic thinking.
Be this as it may, it is hardly surprising that, when Apollinarius, the great champion of Alexandrian orthodoxy,
lapsed in his old age into teaching the heresy of an incomplete human nature in Christ, Antioch produced a
succession of teachers who were concerned to maintain
at all costs the completeness of the Saviour's humanity.
It is also understandable that Alexandria should be
watchful for the least signs of heresy on the part of
Antioch; and when a theologically unimaginative but
critically active Antiochene named Nestorius became
Patriarch of Constantinople in 428 everything was ready
for an explosion. It came when Nestorius openly sup-
ported his chaplain Anastasius in denouncing the application to the Blessed Virgin Mary of the title *theotokos*
or 'Mother of God'. Nestorius's temerity brought upon
him the immediate attention of Cyril, the Patriarch of
Alexandria. With the subsequent details we are not concerned, except to notice that it culminated in the condemnation of Nestorius as a heretic at the Council of
Ephesus in 431.

Whether Nestorius in fact professed the heresy which

has come to be called by his name is unimportant for our present purpose. Since the rediscovery, at the end of the last century, of his long-vanished work *The Bazaar of Heracleides* a number of scholars have formed the opinion that in all probability Nestorius himself never drew from his premises the conclusions which Cyril believed him to have drawn and which were drawn by some of his followers. Nor is it to be supposed that the outlook of Antiochene theology logically implied the Nestorian heresy; Cyril himself recognized the falsity of such a supposition in his reconciliation with John of Antioch in 433. What is true, however, is that, while the pluralistic emphasis of Antioch made it perfectly easy to preserve the distinction of the humanity and the divinity in Christ, it made it very difficult to provide for their real union.

Apollinarius had maintained the union by removing from Christ's humanity one of its constituents, the rational soul, and inserting the divine Logos in its place; and Apollinarius had rightly been condemned at Constantinople. No Antiochene could tolerate such a mutilation; the humanity must remain entire and complete. But how then is the unity of the humanity and the divinity to be effected? If the humanity is complete we shall surely have a complete human individual and it will be this individual and not the divine Logos who will be the subject of Christ's human life. No wonder then, the Alexandrian will reflect, that these Antiochenes refuse to call Mary *theotokos*; they cannot help believing that he whom she bore was not God but a man, even if God came to dwell in him after she had borne him. Whatever they may say, they believe in two Sons, one the Son of God and the other the son of Mary, however close the relation of the two may be. Antioch has preserved the natures from confusion, but it has not united them in any real sense of the term. And if an Antiochene has mercifully stopped short of heresy it can only be because he has stopped short of the logical conclusions from his premises.

What, however, will happen if we refuse to separate the natures? Shall we not have to deny that Christ was really man? Cyril had spoken of 'one incarnate nature of God the Word', in a phrase which, while he believed it to be due to Athanasius, was in fact taken from Apollinarius. And if there is one incarnate nature, it can only be the divine nature, for nothing can happen to that. And if it is the divine nature, then the human nature must have been absorbed into it, if indeed the human nature can be said to have existed at all. Two natures before the union, if you will; but after the union only one, and that divine. Such was the conclusion drawn from Cyril's words by an over-enthusiastic disciple named Eutyches. The union was maintained, but at the expense of confusion. Eutyches and all those who denied the duality of the natures were condemned in 451 by the Council of Chalcedon; to the great jubilation of the Nestorians who seem not to have clearly realized that it impartially condemned them as well.

That Eutyches was a heretic can hardly be denied; that all those who refused to speak of two natures in

Christ were heretics, too, is not so certain. Monophysitism—the assertion that in Christ there is only one
nature and that divine—is a very complex phenomenon,
and it is highly significant that many of the monophysites condemned Eutyches as a heretic, as do their successors in Armenia, Ethiopia and Malabar today. To
many of them it appeared that the Council of Chalcedon
was a Nestorian Council used by a Nestorian govern-
ment to increase the centralized control of the Empire.
It is difficult to see how such an impression can survive
an examination of the definition of faith put out by the
Council, but even to-day one can hear an Armenian
theologian charitably assuring a Byzantine that present-
day Byzantines are not really heretical because they have
providentially been led to interpret the decrees of the
Nestorian Council of Chalcedon in an orthodox monophysite sense; it is not modern Chalcedonians that are
heretical, only the Council of Chalcedon. Certainly the
present-day monophysites are most vehement in insisting that they believe that Christ is truly man, and they
are equally emphatic in condemning Eutyches. Whether
it is heretical to say that there is only one nature in
Christ will clearly depend upon what you mean by the
word 'nature'; if you mean by it what post-Chalce-
donian orthodoxy has meant by 'person' your belief will
be perfectly orthodox, but you will then be left without
a word to denote the humanity and the divinity in
Christ.

Monophysitism was in fact a remarkably fissiparous
and protean movement. Some monophysites were *theo-*

paschites, teaching that, because there was only one nature in Christ and that divine, therefore the Godhead was crucified on Calvary. Some, at the other extreme, were *aphthartodocetists* or 'incorruptibilists', teaching that, because there was only one nature in Christ and that divine, what looked like human nature in him was really only a phantasmal appearance assumed by the incorruptible deity. Some of them, such as John Philoponus, ended up as tritheists. For, they argued, everyone (with the possible exception of the wicked Nestorians) agrees that in Christ there is only one *hypostasis*, and we believe that in him there is only one *physis* or *ousia*. *Hypostasis*, *physis* and *ousia* are therefore identical. But everyone (with the possible exception of the wicked Sabellians) agrees that in the Godhead there are three *hypostases*, so it must follow that there are three *physes* or *ousiai*. The moderate monophysites went to no such lengths. Severus of Antioch, for example, argued firmly against Julian of Halicarnassus and the incorruptibilists; and, in much the same way as Prestige has defended Nestorius against the charge of being a Nestorian,[1] W. A. Wigram has defended Severus against the charge of being really a monophysite.[2]

It is interesting to notice that one of the chief advantages which the Nestorians claimed for their sharp division between the divinity and the humanity in Christ was that, by restricting his sufferings to the man whom the Logos had assumed, they were able, as in their view

---

[1] *Fathers and Heretics*, ch. vi.
[2] *The Separation of the Monophysites*, ch. xi, xiv.

the Alexandrians were not, to preserve the impassibility of the deity. This claim has been somewhat of an embarrassment to most of Nestorius's modern sympathisers, who have been only too anxious to argue in favour of a suffering deity, but in the fifth century it was a very considerable embarrassment to his opponents. We shall see later on how it was to be met. At the moment we may observe that, if Nestorianism is true, we have no justification for giving divine worship to the historic Jesus at all. For, if the ultimate subject of his human activities and experiences is not the uncreated Logos but a man, it is idolatrous to give him divine honour. The Nestorians themselves, it is needless to say, never drew this logical consequence of their theory. But, just as the Arians were prepared to worship the Son as divine while holding him to be only a superior creature, so the Nestorians were prepared to worship Jesus of Nazareth as divine while holding that he was only indwelt by divinity. From this point of view, therefore, we may say that Nestorianism, like Arianism, was infected by a thoroughly pagan readiness to make terms with idolatry. But this does not mean that everyone who accepted the label of Nestorian was a deliberate and formal idolater.

It was the peculiar excellence of the Council of Chalcedon that it explicitly maintained, against Eutychianism on the one side and Nestorianism on the other, the doctrine of the unconfused union of the two natures. In so doing, however, it adopted a form of statement that was on the surface very much more Antiochene than Alexandrian, and this gave some colour to the impression which was received both by Nestorius and the monophysites that, in spite of its personal condemnation of Nestorius, Chalcedon was really a triumph for Nestorianism. But in fact the main influence upon the Council, from the theological point of view, was not Antiochene but Roman. It was the letter which Pope Leo the Great had written in 449 to the Patriarch Flavian of Constantinople that brought such a refreshing Western breeze into the overcharged atmosphere of the Eastern controversies when it was read over two years later to the Chalcedonian fathers. Received with acclamation by them, it became the basis of the Council's definition of faith, though care was taken, in approving Leo's letter, to give pride of place to the synodical epistles of Cyril of Alexandria.

The operative passage of the Definition runs as follows:

> Following, then, the holy Fathers, we all unanimously teach our Lord Jesus Christ one and the same Son, the same perfect in Godhead, the same perfect in manhood, truly God and truly man, the same (consisting) of a rational soul and a body, consubstantial (*homoousion*) with the Father as regards the Godhead and consubstantial with us as regards the manhood, in all things like us except sin; begotten from the Father before the ages as regards the Godhead, the same in these last days for us and for our salvation (born) of Mary the Virgin the *theotokos* as regards the manhood, one and the same Christ, Son, Lord, only-begotten, recognized in two natures, unconfusedly, unchangeably, indivisibly,

inseparably, the distinction of the natures being in no wise abolished by the union, but rather the property of each nature being preserved and concurring into one *prosopon* and one *hypostasis*, not (as if he were) parted or divided into two *prosopa*, but one and the same God, Word, Lord, Jesus Christ.

The central part of this statement is characteristically Antiochene, with its balanced statement of the two parallel natures. But this is sandwiched between two assertions of the unity of the Son, which are no less characteristically Alexandrian. Where the statement is definitely not Alexandrian is in making an analysis of the historic Christ rather than describing the incarnation of the pre-existent Son of God. The tendency of Antioch was always to start from the concrete figure of Jesus of Nazareth as men had known him in the flesh; while Alexandria, from the time of Athanasius and before, was dominated by the thought of the pre-existent creative Logos who had taken human nature for the salvation of man. However, as I have already remarked, the main influence upon the definition was that of Leo of Rome, and it is to his famous letter to Flavian, the 'Tome of Leo', that I shall now turn.

Leo opens his argument with an onslaught upon Eutyches, and it is interesting to observe that there is nothing analytical or formal in this; it is thoroughly 'Alexandrine' and indeed Athanasian.

The same who was the everlasting only-begotten of the everlasting Begetter was born of the Holy Spirit and Mary the Virgin. This temporal birth diminished in no way that divine and eternal birth and added nothing to it, but was entirely concerned with the reparation of man who had been deceived, so that he should conquer death and by his power destroy the devil, who had the power of death. For we should not have been able to overcome the author of sin and death had not he assumed our nature and made it his own, whom neither sin could contaminate nor death detain.

Only when he has expounded this assumption of our human nature by the pre-existent Word does Leo go on to analyse the historic Jesus who results from it. Here he states the parallelism of the two natures without hesitation, but there is always present the realization that they are not on the same footing, since one is uncreated and the other created, one is from all eternity and the other began when the Holy Ghost came upon Mary.

The property, therefore, of each nature being preserved and converging into one Person, humility is assumed by majesty, weakness by power, mortality by eternity, and in order to pay the debt of our condition the inviolable nature was united to a passible nature, so that, as was appropriate for our remedies, one and the same mediator of God and men, the man Jesus Christ, might from the one be able to die and from the other be unable. Thus true God was born in a whole and perfect nature of true man, complete in what was his own and complete in what was ours.

Here is the parallelism, but the transaction is inherently one-sided.

He assumed the form of a servant without the defilement

of sin. *He enriched what was human, but he did not diminish what was divine.*

And this one-sidedness is in fact a direct consequence of the fact that each nature preserves its identity, since divinity and humanity are indefeasibly diverse.

> Each nature retains its own property without defect; and as the form of God does not detract from the form of the servant so the form of the servant does not impair the form of God.

Paradoxical as it may seem, it is precisely because each nature retains its own property without defect that the humanity is enriched while the divinity is undiminished. For it is the very property of created being that it is open to enrichment by its Creator. Nevertheless, the human nature is not destroyed by this exaltation.

> For he who is true God is also true man; and there is nothing false in this unity, while lowliness and the height of deity are mutually related (*invicem sunt*[1]). For, as God is not changed by the compassion (exhibited), so man is not consumed by the dignity (conferred). For each form does what is proper to it in communion with the other; the Word, that is, doing what is proper to the Word, and the flesh performing what is proper to flesh.

It is only when he has given this admirably lucid exposition of the unconfused union of the two natures that Leo goes on to apply it in a way which is, one must admit, open to serious criticism. Immediately after the

---

[1] For the meaning of this phrase see my *Christ, the Christian and the Church*, p. 22, n. 1. Cf. also T. G. Jalland, *St. Leo the Great*, p. 458; R. V. Sellers, *The Council of Chalcedon*, p. 237, n. 5.

words which have just been quoted, he writes, with reference to the Word and the flesh respectively, 'The one of these shines out in miracles, the other succumbs to injuries.' He then develops the point in a famous sequence of antitheses:

> The birth of the flesh is a manifestation of the human nature; the birth from the Virgin is a sign of divine power. The infancy of the babe is shown by the lowliness of the cradle; the greatness of the Most High is declared by the voices of angels. He whom Herod impiously designs to slay is like the very beginnings of men; but he whom the Magi rejoice suppliantly to adore is Lord of all. . . . To hunger, to thirst, to be weary, to sleep is evidently human; but to feed with five loaves thousands of men and to bestow on the Samaritan woman the living water, to draw which would cause her who drank it to thirst no more, and to walk on the surface of the water with unsinking feet and by rebuking the tempest to bring down the upliftings of the waves, is beyond doubt divine. As, then, to cut a long story short, it does not belong to the same nature to weep with feelings of pity over a dead friend and, after the stone had been removed from the tomb where he had been buried for four days, to raise him up alive again by the command of his voice; or to hang on the wood and to make all the elements tremble when day had been turned into night; or to be transfixed by nails and to open the gates of paradise to the faith of the thief; so it does not belong to the same nature to say 'I and my Father are one' and 'My Father is greater than I'. For, although in the Lord Jesus Christ there is one Person of God and man, yet that from which there is a common contumely in both is one thing and that from which there

is a common glory is another. For from what is ours he has the humanity which is less than the Father, and from the Father he has the divinity which is equal to the Father.

Now the first thing that strikes us about this passage is that, while Leo professes to be classifying the activities of the divine Logos under the headings respectively of his humanity and his divinity, all those that he mentions under either head are comprised within the sphere of the incarnate life. We might expect that the activities which fell under the heading of divinity would include those cosmic creative operations by which the Son 'through whom all things were made' sustains the universe in being. There is, however, no mention of these at all. All the activities mentioned are in fact exercised within the sphere of the Incarnation and are mediated through the human nature taken from Mary. Christ uttered the words 'I and my Father are one' with the same lips as the words 'My Father is greater than I'; he walked on the surface of the sea with the same feet that were weary after walking on the roads of Galilee. What Leo has classified as acts of the human and of the divine nature are respectively acts such as any ordinary man could perform and acts which could only be performed by one who was God as well as man. But they are all alike acts performed in the human nature; and we might in some cases find it difficult to decide whether an act which is, as we should say, supranormal is possible to Christ simply in view of his Godhead or in view of his perfect humanity. When, for example, he stills the storm, is he exercising the authority of the Creator or the authority over the lower creation which man lost through the Fall and which is now restored in the Second Adam? It is very hard to know. In view of all this, we can hardly be surprised that some scholars have interpreted the sentence already quoted, which contains the somewhat ambiguous phrase *invicem sunt*, as meaning that in Leo's view, the two natures operate either in separated spheres or alternately.[1] It is perhaps more to the point that at Chalcedon itself, in spite of the general acclamation of Leo's Tome, certain bishops from Illyricum and Palestine objected to some phrases in it as savouring of Nestorianism. Their misgivings were allayed by Aetius of Constantinople, who produced certain similar passages from Cyril. Among these was the following from Cyril's letter to Acacius of Melitene:

> There are some sayings which are in the highest degree God-befitting; others befit manhood; and others there are which, as it were, hold a middle rank, demonstrating that the Son of God is at once God and man.[2]

The inadequacy of Leo's discussion is shown by the fact that he makes no mention at all of this third category of Cyril's, yet it is really the key to the whole matter. For the whole of the incarnate life is the life of God-made-man, and Christ's acts are the acts of God-in-manhood. Some of them may show more clearly than others that the personal subject of these acts is not a man but God; none of them, however, are acts of the divine nature

---

[1] Thus Bindley, *The Oecumenical Documents of the Faith*, 2nd. ed., p. 227, translates 'have their separate spheres'.

[2] P.G. lxxvii, 196; quoted by Sellers, op. cit., p. 247.

operating independently of the manhood, for any such acts would, like the act by which the divine Word sustains the universe, fall outside the sphere of the Incarnate life altogether. In fact, all the acts of the incarnate life are *theandric*, acts of a divine Person in a human nature; the point had been made perfectly clear long before the time of Leo in a letter (the fourth) of Athanasius to Serapion the importance of which is pointed out by Prestige.

The relevant passage begins very much in the style of Leo:

> Therefore, since God he is and man he became, as God he raised the dead and, healing all by a word, also changed the water into wine. Such deeds were not those of a man. But as wearing a body he thirsted and was wearied and suffered; these experiences are not characteristic of the deity. And as God he said, 'I am in the Father and the Father in me'; but as wearing a body he rebuked the Jews, 'Why do you seek to kill me, a man that has told you the truth which I heard from the Father?'

But now comes the non-Leonine qualification:

> But these facts did not occur in dissociation, on lines governed by the particular quality of the several acts, so as to ascribe one set of experiences to the body apart from the deity and the other to the deity apart from the body. *They all occurred interconnectedly*, and it was one Lord who did them all wondrously by his own grace. For he spat in human fashion, yet his spittle was charged with deity, for therewith he caused the eyes of the man born blind to recover their sight; and when he willed to declare himself God it

was with a human tongue that he signified this, saying, 'I and the Father are one'. And he used to perform cures by a mere act of will. But he stretched forth a human hand to raise Peter's wife's mother when she was sick of a fever, and to raise up from the dead the daughter of the ruler of the synagogue when she had already expired.[1]

Two points remain to be added. The first is that Leo, in spite of his over-simplified analysis, had no difficulty in making it clear that he was no Nestorian.[2] The second and more important is that the definition of Chalcedon, in spite of its obvious debt to the Tome of Leo, altogether ignores the passages which have just been quoted.

2. THE IMPLICATIONS OF CHALCEDON

Thus, against the errors of both Nestorianism and Eutychianism, the Council of Chalcedon affirmed the Church's doctrine of the Incarnation in formulas which have been accepted by the central tradition of Christendom as normative down to the present day. In Christ there are two natures, a divine and a human, inhering in one divine Person in unconfused union. Chalcedon has in recent years received somewhat rough treatment even in sympathetic quarters. Archbishop William Temple, while applauding its affirmation of the central fact, described it as representing 'the bankruptcy of Greek patristic theology'.[3] Prestige laid stress upon its negative

---

[1] *Fathers and Heretics*, p. 369. Cf. Prestige's own comments, pp. 238, 331.
[2] Cf. Sellers, op. cit., p. 228f.
[3] *Christus Veritas*, p. 134.

and formal character. 'In defining the two natures', he wrote, 'it speaks positively. But in defining their relations it speaks negatively. . . . The formula states admirably what Christ is not.'[1] 'How negative and abstract the Chalcedonian settlement was, is shown by the subsequent history of Christological discussion. . . . Proof of its incapacity was several times repeated during the next two centuries, as successive efforts were undertaken to reconcile adherents and opponents of Chalcedonian phraseology.'[2] And again:

> The further the analysis is pursued of each nature, taken in abstraction, the harder it becomes for the most orthodox Chalcedonian to avoid the very difficulties in which Nestorius was engulfed, and the less content is left for the actual personality which was embodied in both natures. At best, Jesus Christ disappears in the smoke-screen of the two-nature philosophy. Formalism triumphs, and the living figure of the evangelical Redeemer is desiccated to a logical mummy. The monophysites were horrified by the barren intellectual desert into which the gateway of Chalcedon opened, and fought raggedly but persistently to gain a more realistic outlet for Christology. The orthodox had their choice between two unsatisfactory alternatives: either they kept the gateway shut, and occupied their minds with pursuits less paralysing to the heart than speculative theology now threatened to become; or else, like the great Maximus the Confessor, while continuing to refine their definitions they ignored the practical bearing of them, and drawing on the thought of Cyril, whose religious fertility still lay stored beneath the barren turf of formal logic, and of the pseudo-

[1] Op. cit., p. 298.   [2] Ibid., p. 299.

Dionysius, a Christian Neoplatonist of monophysite lean-
ings, they preached a richer Gospel than had strict warrant
in the admonitory negations actually delivered under pres-
sure from the untheological West at the Council of Chalcedon.[1]

This is a serious indictment, and it must be admitted that
the formal analysis of the Chalcedonian statement looks
somewhat bleak and arid by the side of the Creeds of
Nicaea and Constantinople which Chalcedon so en-
thusiastically endorsed, with their triumphant proclama-
tion of the only-begotten consubstantial Son of God,
who for us men and for our salvation came down from
heaven and was incarnate by the Holy Ghost of the
Virgin Mary and was made man, or by the side of the
concrete Cyrilline affirmation of the one incarnate
nature of God the Word. It is only too easy to represent
the later story of Chalcedonian orthodoxy as a successive
trimming down of Apollinarianism until nothing is left.
Apollinarius mutilated the humanity of its rational soul
and was condemned for doing so. Chalcedon said that
Christ had a complete human nature, but no human
person. What does this mean in concrete fact? Perhaps
that there is no human energy or operation, suggest the
monergists. Perhaps that there is no human will, suggest
the monothelites. No, replies Chalcedonian orthodoxy,
either of these views will mutilate the human nature. So
the monergists and the monothelites were condemned
in 681 at the Third Council of Constantinople, the sixth
ecumenical. Nothing human is missing in Christ except

[1] Ibid., p. 301.

a human person or *hypostasis*; and the absence of a human person does not mutilate the nature, for 'person' is not the name of a constituent of human nature, it is a purely metaphysical term. Nestorianism has been avoided, but by depersonalizing human nature. Has not the evangelical Redeemer, in Prestige's words, been desiccated to a logical mummy?

In the face of such criticisms as these, it is pleasant to be able to note that at least one recent writer of unquestionable competence has come down unhesitatingly in defence of Chalcedon, namely Dr. R. V. Sellers in his recent work *The Council of Chalcedon*. On this crucial point of the impersonal humanity he writes as follows:

> Certainly, 'an impersonal manhood' is an unfortunate phrase, which, anti-Nestorian in purpose, means no more than that the manhood had no independent existence; it does not mean that the manhood was deprived of its properties in its union with Godhead, but, as it implies, that these were exercised not separately but in the *hypostasis* of the Logos, who united the manhood to himself and made it his own. All this—which is implicit in the Chalcedonian statement that 'the difference of the natures was not abolished by reason of the union, but the properties of each were preserved'—is brought out by later teachers in their insistence against the monothelites that, while having its existence in the Person of the Logos, his manhood possessed its quality of self-determination.[1]

It must be admitted that the term 'impersonal manhood' is ambiguous. It does not in fact occur in the defi-

[1] Op. cit., p. 345.

nition of Chalcedon, and in any case many of those who have attacked Chalcedonian Christology on the strength of it seem to have entirely misunderstood what it meant to Chalcedonians. It does not mean that the manhood lacks a human soul, or a human will, or any other component of human nature; the 'person' which it declares to be absent is not a psychological or physical entity, but a metaphysical one. On the other hand the term does not mean that the human nature of Christ is miraculously suspended in a kind of metaphysical vacuum without inhering in any metaphysical subject at all, as if (to use an illustration from geometrical optics) it was something like a virtual image formed by a spherical mirror. On the contrary it means that the human nature inheres in the Person of the pre-existent divine Word; the human nature does not lack a person, but only a person other than the Word. In one sense, therefore, it is as personal as it could be, and in fact *more personal* (if the term may be allowed) than any other human nature that has ever existed or will exist. For it is ultimately grounded not in a finite *hypostasis*, but in the infinite uncreated *hypostasis* or Person of God the Son. This truth was given clear expression by the sixth-century theologian Leontius of Byzantium, whose importance was stressed as long ago as 1917 by Dr. H. M. Relton in his *Study in Christology* and has more recently been re-emphasized by Dr. Sellers. Leontius himself was strongly influenced by the Aristotelian revival which seems to have been a feature of his time, but his essential contribution to Christology does not rest upon any

philosophical doctrine. Arguing against the monophysites, he accepted their assertion that a nature cannot
exist without a *hypostasis*. But he refused to accept either
the Nestorian consequence that since Christ has a
human nature he must have a human *hypostasis* in addition to his divine *hypostasis* or the monophysite consequence that since he has no human *hypostasis* he cannot
have a human nature. The human nature of Christ is
neither unattached to a *hypostasis* nor does it inhere in a
human *hypostasis*; it inheres in the divine *hypostasis* of
the Second Person of the Holy Trinity. It is neither itself
a *hypostasis* nor is it *anhypostatic*, but it is *enhypostatic* in
the divine Word. The fundamental wonder and mystery
of the Incarnation is that it is possible for a created
nature, without being destroyed or absorbed, to inhere
in an uncreated Person. Formal and analytic as it may
appear at first sight, Leontius's doctrine of the *enhypostasia* is in its essence nothing else than the Athanasian and
Cyrilline doctrine, that in the Incarnation the Logos did
not simply come and dwell in a man who already existed
but himself *became man*. Dr. Sellers has pertinently
quoted passages from both Cyril and Leo which mean
neither more nor less than this.

> Scripture does not say [writes Cyril in his second letter to
> Nestorius] that the Logos united to himself the *prosōpon* of
> a man, but that 'he became flesh'. But this expression, 'the
> Word became flesh' is nothing else than that he became
> partaker of flesh and blood, just as we do, and made our
> body his own.

And this, from the Tome of Leo:

We should not have been able to overcome the author of sin and death had he [*sc.* the Son] not taken our nature and made it his own.[1]

He took our nature and made it his own—this is a precise statement of the doctrine of the *enhypostasia*.

The temptation to draw parallels between different truths of the Faith is a dangerous one and needs to be strictly disciplined; the following may however be illuminating. We saw in the last chapter, in considering the doctrine of the Holy Trinity, how the notion of derived equality, which the Church was obliged to formulate in order to avoid the errors of modalism, tritheism and subordinationism, was saved from becoming formal and analytical by the notion of *perichōrēsis*. In the present chapter, in considering the doctrine of the Incarnation, we have seen that the notion of unconfused union, which the Church was obliged to formulate to avoid the mutually opposed errors of Eutychianism and Nestorianism, was saved from becoming formal and analytical by the notion of *enhypostasia*. In each case we have an earlier phase in which the orthodox Christian doctrine tends to be generally stated in what might be loosely described as dynamic terms. In the one case the unoriginate Father is thought of as eternally begetting the Son and spirating the Spirit; in the other case the Son is thought of as uniting manhood to himself and becoming man. (We must, of course, remember that the process in the Trinity takes place in the eternal and uncreated realm, while the process in the Incarnation takes

[1] Sellers, op. cit., p. 319, 320.

place in the temporal and created.) Then in each case there arise two types of heresies; one which confuses the terms of the process, the other which isolates them from one another. Thus in Triadology modalism confuses the Persons, while subordinationism and tritheism separate them. In Christology Eutychianism confuses the natures, while Nestorianism separates them. The Church's reaction in each case is to state a doctrine which preserves both the distinction and the union between the terms. So we get the Cappadocian Triadology and the Leonine Christology; and in each case the doctrine becomes, as it were, solidified in static and quasi-logical formulas. Finally, the concrete profundity and dynamism of the Christian truth is recovered by the introduction of an organic concept, that of *perichōrēsis* in the first case, that of *enhypostasia* in the second. This account of the matter is, it need hardly be said, over-simplified and, like some of the systems which it discusses, formalistic. Were it completely adequate, we could have summarized both our Triadology and our Christology in the same formula, and should not have needed notions so contrasted as that of derived equality in the first case and unconfused union in the latter. History refuses to conform to schematic patterns, and in any case Triadology is one thing and Christology is another. We have already seen how over-ingenious thinkers have come to grief through over-assimilating the two. Nevertheless, provided that due care is taken, the comparison is not without significance; I shall resist the temptation to follow it any further.

In the Leonine and Chalcedonian formulations there is, as we have seen, a formal parallelism between the two natures of Christ. In Leo's words:

Each nature retains its own property without defect; and as the form of God does not detract from the form of the servant so the form of the servant does not impair the form of God.

With this parallelism there is, however, an essential diversity. For the divine nature is uncreated and eternal, while the human nature is created and temporal. Even in the statement of the parallelism this disparity becomes clear. 'The same perfect in Godhead, the same perfect in manhood', declares Chalcedon, 'truly God and truly man, . . . consubstantial with the Father as regards the Godhead and consubstantial with us as regards the manhood'; the two limbs of the successive conjunctions are isomorphic in their structure. However, in the succeeding phrases the essential disparity begins to appear beneath the verbal isomorphism. 'Begotten from the Father before the ages as regards the Godhead, the same in these last days for us and for our salvation of Mary the Virgin the *theotokos* as regards the manhood'— what kind of parallelism is this between what goes on in uncreated eternity and what happened in the created realm at one particular moment of time? And when the definition concludes by stating the unity of the Person all parallelism and isomorphism is abandoned. The distinction of the two natures is in no wise abolished and the property of each is preserved, but they concur into one *prosōpon* and *hypostasis*, and this *prosōpon* is not human but divine: 'one and the same God, Word, Lord, Jesus Christ.' The word 'man' is here conspicuously absent.[1] We have in fact returned through very different wording to the fundamental one-sidedness of the Nicene-Constantiopolitan Creed, which itself was explicitly ratified by Chalcedon. The only-begotten Son of the Father, consubstantial with him from all eternity and to all eternity in derived equality, has come down from heaven for us men and for our salvation, has been born of the Holy Ghost and the Virgin Mary and has been made man. In the Incarnate Lord there is a certain parallelism between the divine and the human nature as they inhere in the one Person; but, since the Person is divine, and in God nature and Person are substantially identical, the union of the natures is an assumption of human nature by God and is not an assumption of divinity by a man. In that typically Western document the *Quicunque vult* the parallelism breaks down in much the same way. 'He is God from the substance of the Father, begotten before the worlds; and he is man from the substance of his mother, born in the world. Perfect God, and perfect man (subsisting from a rational soul and human flesh). Equal to the Father as regards the divinity, less than the Father as regards the humanity.

[1] Thus Professor V. Lossky writes, summarizing St. John of Damascus: 'In one self-same act, the Word assumed human nature, gave it existence and deified it. The humanity which was assumed and appropriated by the Person of the Son receives its being in the divine hypostasis; it did not previously exist as a distinct nature, it did not enter into union with God, but it appears from the start as the human nature of the Word' (*Théologie mystique de l'Église d'Orient*, p. 137).

Who, although he be God and man, nevertheless there are not two but one Christ.' Verbally the parallelism is maintained, though the pairing of *ante saecula* with *in saeculo* and of *aequalis* with *minor* shows that it is at least as much a contrast as a parallel. 'He is one', yes, but '*not* by the conversion of Godhead into flesh, *but* by the assumption of manhood into God'. Here the asymmetry is explicit. God has become man; a man has not become God.

It is for this reason that the word 'theandric' has been used to describe the operations and activities of the incarnate Lord. The word must not be taken to imply that the human and divine natures have been compounded into one hybrid 'theandric' nature, or that the divine and human operations have been compounded into some intermediate type of operation. All the activities and operations of the Word as incarnate are operations of the human nature, not of the divine nature or of some nature which is neither human nor divine. But they are operations of a human nature which is enhypostatized in a divine Person, and so their ultimate metaphysical agent is not a man but God. This point will stand out even more clearly when we have paid attention to the fact that the union of humanity with divinity in Christ takes place not in the divine nature as such but in the divine Person.

3. UNITY IN THE PERSON

In God, we have said, nature and Person are substantially identical; and what else can we say, since God *is* all that he *has*? In him there are neither accidents nor mutability. Yet there is a danger ahead. Was it not the identification of nature with person, of *physis* with *hypostasis*, that led John Philoponus from monophysitism into tritheism? Are not, in fact, both tritheists and modalists agreed upon this identification? One nature, therefore one Person, say the modalists. Three Persons, therefore three natures, say the tritheists. In answer to this objection we must point out the force of the word 'substantially'. It is not used merely rhetorically, as is so often the case in modern speech. It means what it says: in God nature and Person are identical as regards their *substantia* or *ousia*. But in working out this point we must make reference to two other theological themes. The first is the doctrine of the divine Persons as subsistent relations; it was briefly discussed in the last chapter. The second is the doctrine that the union of humanity with divinity in Christ takes place in the divine Person of the Son, and not in the divine nature. Stated thus baldly, these may seem to be typically arid scholastic formulas, calculated to make our religion as frigid and sapless as themselves; but when we see what they are concerned to preserve, we shall, I think, find that it is something that lies at the heart of our Life in and with Christ.

The central point of St. Augustine's doctrine of the divine Persons as subsistent relations is that it provides for something other than substance in God. As the Saint of Hippo clearly shows, if the only categories available for use are substance and accident, we shall have to identify Person with substance, for there are no accidents in God. And then either the unity of substance will lead us into modalism or the triplicity of Persons will lead us into tritheism. There may perhaps be other ways of establishing the point at issue than by the adoption of categories of the Aristotelian logic, but somehow or other the point has to be made. And St. Augustine's transposition of relation from the sub-class of accidents into the sub-class whose other member is substance is one way of doing it. But here we need more than ever to remember the caveat which I emphasized in the last chapter; that in adopting into theology terms and concepts from non-theological disciplines we must apply them not univocally but analogically, and must look to the theological realm for their new shade of meaning or *modus significandi*. Thus understood, the doctrine enables us to maintain that the Father is God and the Son is God and the Holy Ghost is God; while the Father is not the Son, nor the Son the Holy Ghost, nor the Holy Ghost the Father. Then by introducing our second principle, that the union takes place not in the nature but in the Person, we can consistently go on to affirm that, while God became man in Jesus Christ, it was God the Son who became man, and not God the Father or God the Holy Ghost. The Person of the Son is substantially identical with the divine nature or essence, but the human nature is not united directly to the divine nature —for in that case the whole trinity of Persons would be incarnate—but to the Person of the Son. The point has been clearly stated in the following passage from the modern Jesuit theologian Père Paul Galtier:

Strictly speaking, the only direct union which we are obliged to admit is that of the human nature and the divine Person. The union which we also affirm between the natures themselves is only, as it were, the consequence of this. It results from the double fact of their common possession by the same Person and of the real identity which exists between this Person and the divine nature; this identity does not allow of the Person's uniting to itself a second nature without uniting the latter, in a certain way, to its first nature. But, on the other hand, this very identity does not prevent there being between the Person and its first nature a distinction which allows us to conceive and say of the one what we cannot conceive and say of the other. The mystery of the Holy Trinity implies many distinctions and contrasts of this kind. Many affirmations are true of the Persons which are not true of the nature; and what rules out any formal contradiction is the distinction which forces itself upon our mind between each of the Persons and the divinity which is common to them.[1]

It is important to keep in mind the fact that the unity takes place in the Person when we consider the theory of the *communicatio idiomatum* or interchange of concepts (*antidosis tōn idiōmatōn* or *antidosis tōn onomatōn*). This has sometimes been thought to be nothing more than a piece of linguistic elaboration, but it rests upon a profound theological truth. The linguistic part of the theory is the convention that persons are named by concrete nouns, but natures by abstract ones. The divine nature is thus called 'divinity' or 'Godhead', and the human nature is called 'humanity' or 'manhood'. What con-

[1] *L'Unité du Christ*, p. 97.

crete name are we to give to the divine Person of the
incarnate Word? Clearly we can call him 'God', but can
we call him 'man'? Yes, says the theory, because the
divine Person is directly united to a human nature and is
that nature's subject. Since the Incarnation the Son can
be named both 'God' and 'man'; there is only one
Christ, as Chalcedon insisted. And because this doubly
named Person is the subject of two natures, we can use
either name of him when we describe what he does in
each. Not only can we say that man suffered in the
Crucifixion; we can say that God suffered, too—meaning that he suffered in the manhood which he took from
his mother. And not only can we say that God sustains
the universe; we can say that man, the man Christ Jesus,
sustains it, too—meaning that he sustains it in the Godhead which he possessed from all eternity from the
Father. On the other hand, since the two natures are not
united directly with each other, but mediately through
the direct union of each with the Person, we cannot
predicate of one nature the properties or activities of the
other. Although we can say that God suffered, meaning
that he who is both God and man suffered in his manhood, we cannot say that the Godhead or divinity suffered. And, although we can say that man sustains the
universe, meaning that he who is both man and God
sustains it in his Godhead, we cannot say that his manhood or humanity sustains it. By the attribution to either
personal name of the properties of both natures we
maintain the unity of the Person; by refusing to attribute
the properties of either nature to the other we maintain

the distinction of the natures. And in case this linguistic theory seems to be a reduction of the Redeemer to the status of an exercise in formal logic, here is a verse from a popular Christmas hymn which provides a precise example of its application:

> O wonder of wonders, which none can unfold:
> The Ancient of days is an hour or two old;
> The Maker of all things is made of the earth,
> Man is worshipped by angels, and God comes to birth:
> *Then let us adore him, and praise his great love:*
> *To save us poor sinners he came from above.*

And let us emphasize again that, so far from the human element in Christ suffering any limitation or curtailment from the absence of a human person, the precise opposite is the case. The humanity of Christ fails to personalize itself in a human person not because anything is lacking in it, but because it has been exalted to the stupendous dignity of being personalized (*enhypostatized*) in the Person of God the Son. As St. Thomas says:

> the nature which is assumed does not lack its own personality because of the absence of anything which belongs to the completeness of human nature, but because of the addition of something which is above human nature, namely union with a divine Person.[1]

And in commenting upon a somewhat rash remark attributed to Innocent III to the effect that 'the Person of God has consumed the person of the man', he makes this remarkable assertion:

[1] *S. Theol.*, III, iv, 2 *ad* 2.

This 'consumption' does not mean the destruction of something which formerly existed, but the prevention of something which would otherwise have been. For, *if the human nature had not been assumed by the divine Person, the human nature would have had its own personality.* And to this extent one Person is said, although improperly, to have consumed the other, because by its union the divine Person prevents the human nature from having its own personality.[1]

And here is Père Galtier's comment on St. Thomas:

We can see that the thought of St. Thomas as to what makes a complete and concrete human nature into a person is as clear as it is firm. In Christ there is lacking none of those elements which would otherwise be sufficient to constitute an *hypostasis* or person. In becoming a person, *as it would if it was abandoned by the Word*, it would acquire nothing that it did not possess before. Left to itself, it would cease to be a part in order to become a whole and, by that very fact, it would find that it was a person. If, as certain 'authorities' have said, 'the divine Person in Christ has consumed the human person', this is not in the strict sense of the suppression of something real in it; it is only in the improper sense that in uniting it to itself it has prevented it from being a person. Thus the union with a whole, a whole more noble and perfect, namely the divine Person, is the only thing that prevents the nature from being a Person.[2]

We may perhaps wonder whether Archbishop William Temple recognized how close he was to St. Thomas when he wrote the following passage in 1924:

If we imagine the divine Word withdrawn from Jesus of Nazareth, as the Gnostics believed to have occurred before

---

[1] Ibid., *ad* 3.   [2] Op. cit., p. 191 (italics mine).

the Passion, I think that there would be left, not nothing at all, but a man. Yet this human personality is actually the self-expression of the Eternal Son, so that as we watch the human life, we become aware that it is the vehicle of a divine life, and that the human personality of Jesus Christ is subsumed in the Divine Person of the Creative Word.[1]

Temple's Christology seems in fact to have been a good deal more traditional than either he or most of his contemporaries were aware. He vigorously rejected the Kenotic theory which was so popular at the time, according to which the Incarnation involved that 'God the Eternal Son at a moment of time divested himself of omniscience and omnipotence in order to live a human life, reassuming these attributes at the Ascension'.[2] 'The difficulties', he says, 'are intolerable.'[3] He held that 'God the Son did most truly live the life recorded in the Gospel, but added this to the other work of God'.[4] He was, moreover, emphatic—and this is most important— about the difference between the theological sense of 'person' and the modern psychological sense of 'personality', which he identified, at least in one place,[5] with 'will'. 'I should not hesitate', he said, 'to speak of the human personality of Christ. But that personality does not exist side by side with the divine personality; it is subsumed in it.'[6] Whether Temple really intended to imply that the created psychological will of Christ was absorbed into the divine being may very well be doubted; it appears from the context that we should be

[1] *Christus Veritas*, p. 150.   [2] Ibid., p. 141.   [3] Ibid., p. 142.
[4] Ibid., p. 143.   [5] Ibid., p. 150. Cf. p. 136.   [6] Ibid., p. 150.

justified in interpreting Temple's use of 'subsumed' with the same charitable tolerance which St. Thomas applied to Pope Innocent's use of the similar word 'consumed'. I cannot, however, feel that our understanding of the Incarnation is very much helped by Temple's anxiety to dispose of the metaphysical aspects of the question and concentrate upon the psychological implications; though it must be admitted that he took the metaphysical questions very much more seriously than most contemporary Christologists took them. I should certainly not want to rule them out of consideration, but I am convinced that the early Church was right in seeing the problem of the Incarnation as primarily a metaphysical one. I am frankly amazed to find how often the problem of the Incarnation is taken as simply the problem of describing the mental life and consciousness of the Incarnate Lord, for this problem seems to me to be strictly insoluble. If I am asked what I conceive to be the metaphysical relation between the human and the divine in Christ, I can at least make some sort of attempt at an answer; but if I am asked to say what I believe it feels like to be God incarnate I can only reply that I have not the slightest idea and I should not expect to have it. Nor would I admit that, in saying this, I am substituting a cold and detached academic interest for the warmth of personal Christian devotion; quite the opposite. The two fundamental facts about my relation to Christ are that he evokes from me that consciousness of absolute and unconditional allegiance and adoration that no one but God can rightly claim, and that he and he alone restores me to union with the God from whom my sins have estranged me. That Christ is Lord, and that he is the one Mediator between God and man, are the fundamental facts of the Christian religion; and they are altogether primary and anterior to any questions about the content of his psychological personality. And it is these facts that demand from us the confession that in Christ manhood and Godhead are united without confusion. That we are here confronted with a most profound mystery we should be only too eager to admit; what could be more amazing than that the Creator should become the subject of a created nature which can exist at all only as completely dependent on him?

> *Beata mater munere,*
> *cujus supernus artifex,*
> *mundum pugillo continens,*
> *ventris sub arca clausus est.*

No one is more insistent upon this than the Angelic Doctor.

> The manner in which Christ has united human nature to himself, as an instrument effective for man's salvation, is inexpressible by us (*nobis ineffabilis*) and exceeds every other union of God with a creature.[1]

And again:

> We must now speak of the mystery of the Incarnation, which of all the works of God most greatly surpasses our reason; for nothing more wonderful could be thought of

[1] *Comp. Theol.*, I, 211.

that God could do than that very God, the Son of God, should become very man.[1]

Even the classical comparison between the union of manhood with God in the Incarnation and the union of soul with body in human nature is pronounced not only to be inadequate, but as leading straight to heresy if its inadequacy is not recognized.[2] All that we can say, I think, is that it is the very insufficiency of creaturely being to sustain itself that is the basis of the possibility of its assumption by God. For at the very heart of the creature is God's presence of immensity, the incessant act by which he pours into it its whole being and substance. To be a finite nature is to be *from* God and *to* God: *esse est a Deo et ad Deum esse*. If then a finite nature, by its very finitude, is a pure recipient of the divine activity and a pure dependent upon the divine support, may it not therefore be capable of receiving a further influx of creative power, by which it will be elevated from mere dependence upon God to become, as it were, God's personal instrument and fleshly integument? Just because it is nothing apart from God, may it not be capable of becoming in his hands what it could never be if (*per impossible*) it had an independent reality? And may we not say that in the act of pure obedience to the divine will which received vocal expression in Mary's *Fiat voluntas tua*, human nature was making voluntary and articulate that pure dependence upon God which was

[1] *S.c.G.*, IV, xxvii.
[2] *De Veritate*, xx, 1c. Cf. my *Christ, the Christian and the Church*, p. 9.

the necessary precondition to its elevation to hypostatic union?

> On golden airs—by him upheld—
> She knelt, a soft subjection mute,
> A hushed Dependence, tranced and spelled,
> Still yearning towards the Absolute.
>
> She was a sea-shell from the deep
> Of God; her function this alone,
> Of him to whisper as in sleep
> In everlasting undertone.[1]

At this point in our thought the language of theological discussion perforce gives way to the silence of contemplative adoration. Enough should at least have been said to make it plain how closely Christian devotion is bound up with the doctrine of the unconfused union of the divine and human natures in the one Person of God the Eternal Word and Son.

---

[1] Aubrey de Vere, *Ancilla Domini*.

IV

DEIFIED CREATUREHOOD
THE DOCTRINE OF GRACE

I. THE CATHOLIC DOCTRINE AND THE ALTERNATIVES

As we saw in the first chapter, the orthodox Christian
doctrine about the beings of which the world is composed is that they are *dependent realities*; they are neither,
on the one hand, unsubstantial phantoms or hallucina-
tions nor, on the other, have they that independent and
self-subsistent reality which is the peculiar property of
God himself. We must now consider the remarkable
fact that, in spite of its insistence upon the radical and
indestructible difference of kind that distinguishes the
Creator from even the most exalted of his creatures,
there is a persistent tradition in Christian thought which
finds it impossible to do justice to the transformation
that a human being undergoes when he is incorporated
into Christ except by saying that he is *deified*. The scrip-
tural basis for this way of speaking is to be found in the
Second Epistle of St. Peter, where it is asserted that God
has 'granted to us his precious and exceeding great
promises, that through these ye may become partakers
of the divine nature', *hina . . . genēsthe theias koinōnoi*

physeōs.[1] 'By the time of Origen, . . .' Dr. H. E. W.
Turner tells us, 'the terminology of Deification has
passed firmly and finally into the Christian tradition.'[2]
St. Athanasius states quite categorically that the Word
'became man in order that we might become God'.[3] He
is followed by St. Augustine in the words which are
echoed in the prayer with which the water is blessed at
Mass in the Roman rite: 'He became partaker of our
mortality; he makes us partakers of his divinity,'[4] and in
the assertion 'God wishes to make you a god, not by
nature but by . . . adoption. . . . Thus the whole man is
deified'.[5] Passing from Egypt and Africa of the patristic
age to Spain of the Counter-Reformation, we find St.
John of the Cross describing the summit of Christian
mystical experience by saying that 'the substance of this
soul . . . is God by participation in God'.[6] Nevertheless,
it is made perfectly clear that this deification of the
human being by the grace of God does not in any way
involve the destruction of his creaturedly status. Thus
St. Augustine writes: 'Those who think that we shall be
brought so far as to be changed into the substance of God
and be made altogether what he is must support their
opinion as they may; for my part I do not believe it.'[7]

[1] 2 Pet. i. 4.
[2] *The Patristic Doctrine of Redemption*, p. 81.
[3] *Autos gar enēnthrōpēsen hina hēmeis theopoiēthōmen* (*De Inc.* 54).
[4] *Factus est particeps mortalitatis nostrae; fecit nos participes divinitatis suae* (*De. Trin.*, IV, ii, 4).
[5] *Deus deum te vult facere, non natura sed . . . adoptione . . . Sic totus homo deificatus* (Serm. 166, 4).
[6] *Living Flame*, 2nd ed., II, 34 (Peers, III, p. 158).
[7] *De Nat. et Grat.*, 37.

And in the very sentence from St. John of the Cross from which I have just quoted we are told that 'the substance of this soul . . . is not the substance of God, for into this it cannot be substantially changed'. It is clear from this and from many other passages which might be cited from Christian writers of undoubted orthodoxy that what we are concerned with here is a doctrine of grace as bringing about a state of *deified creaturehood*, and that this is distinct from those doctrines on the one side which would allow for such an entitative transformation into the divine substance as would result in a loss of creaturehood altogether, and from those doctrines on the other side which hold that creaturehood is inherently incapable of deification.

The first type of doctrine which is excluded—namely that of a destruction of the creaturely status—must be clearly distinguished from pantheism in the strict sense. Pantheism is the doctrine that creatures, including man, are identical with God from the first moment of their existence. What we are concerned with here is a doctrine which, while admitting that by their creation human beings are dependent and not self-subsistent realities, would assert the possibility of their subsequently acquiring divine independence and self-subsistence. Admittedly it may not always be easy in practice to distinguish between these two types of belief; a man may not be very clear—and still less may his hearers and readers be—whether he is trying to acquire a status which he did not possess before or trying to become more fully conscious of a status which he already possesses. Again, it is always possible that an orthodox Christian mystic, in his attempts to describe an experience which is by his own admission ineffable, may slip into language which seems to imply a simple and literal entitative conversion of the creature into the Creator. Thus, for example, it is by no means easy to decide whether such controversial figures in the history of Christian spirutality as the fourteenth-century mystics Eckhart and Tauler held a view of creation that was fundamentally pantheistic or a view of mystical union as consisting in a loss of creaturehood, or whether indeed they were perfectly orthodox Christian mystics who were betrayed into incautious and exaggerated language in their attempts to describe their intense consciousness of what I have called deified creaturehood. Even Ruysbroeck was violently attacked as a heretic by Gerson after his death. Yet it was Ruysbroeck who had campaigned against the excesses of Bloemardinne and who could write as follows:

> By union we become one same spirit, one same love, one same life with him, but we remain always creatures. For although transformed in his light and ravished by his love, we recognise and feel that we are other than he.[1]

Or again:

> St. Paul . . . said that he desired to be released from his body and to be with Christ. But he did not say that he wished to be Christ himself, nor God, as now some faithless and perverted men do, who say that they have no God,

---

[1] *Mirror of Eternal Salvation*, c. 19, qu. by a Benedictine of Stanbrook, *Mediaeval Mystical Tradition and St. John of the Cross*, p. 129.

for they have died to themselves, and are united with God so that they have become God.[1]

Or once more:

We cannot issue out of ourselves into God and lose our created nature; and so we must remain everlastingly different from God, and remain created creatures. For no creature can become God, nor can God become any creature.[2]

It is amusing to reflect that, if one wished to be maliciously literal, it would be easier to interpret the last sentence as denying the possibility of both deification and the Incarnation than as being compatible with the heresies of which Ruysbroeck has been suspected. It is clear, however, when we take such passages as these in the context of his work as a whole, that what he is expressing is a doctrine of deification which does not involve the suppression of creaturehood.

Just what is involved in this central Christian tradition of deified creaturehood or creaturely deification we shall have to consider later on. At the moment it will be well to remark that it has not been threatened only by a view which stresses deification to the point at which the creature ceases to be a creature, but also by a view which stresses creaturehood to the point at which deification becomes impossible. And just as the former view can be found both inside and outside Christendom, so can the latter. Its most conspicuous manifestation is in certain sections of Reformation Protestantism, but before turn-

---

[1] *Werken*, III, p. 276-8, qu. by E. Colledge in Introduction to *The Spiritual Espousals*, p. 28.
[2] *Werken*, IV, p. 31, qu. by Colledge, ibid.

ing to these, it may be illuminating to see how the problem has arisen in connection with the mystical trend in Islam which goes by the name of Sufism.

There is one aspect of the problem of mystical grace in Islam with which we are not directly concerned, namely whether, on grounds of Christian doctrine, genuine mystical experience of the supernatural order in Islam is possible. This question has been canvassed a good deal in recent years, especially among Roman Catholic theologians, and there seems to be general agreement that, while non-Christian religion is not on the whole likely to rise very much above the natural level, God is able to give his graces as and where he sees fit, and it is only to be expected that, wherever men and women sincerely and honestly seek after God, he will not leave them helpless and stranded. The Roman Church has explicitly condemned the proposition that no grace is vouchsafed outside the Church[1] and it is a theological commonplace that God does not withhold grace from a man who does what he can.[2] It must furthermore be remembered that, as Dr. Margaret Smith has shown,[3] there were very considerable contacts between Christianity and Mohammedanism in the early Islamic period, and some of the Muslim mystics were undoubtedly influenced by Christian ideas. Especially this appears to be true of the tenth-century mystic al-Hallaj, whose case

[1] In the bull *Unigenitus* of 1713; Denzinger, 1379: *Extra Ecclesiam nulla conceditur gratia.*
[2] *Facienti quod in se est Deus non denegat gratiam.*
[3] *Studies in Early Mysticism in the Near and Middle East.*

has been studied in detail by M. Louis Massignon and Père Joseph Maréchal;[1] the general problem has been fully discussed by Otto Karrer in the chapter on 'Revelation Outside the Visible Church' in his book *Religions of Mankind*. We are not however concerned with the compatibility of Islamic mysticism with Christian theology but with its compatibility with Islamic theology, and it is a remarkable fact that the existence of Islamic mystics has been much more of a scandal to the mind of Islam than to that of Christendom.

The essence of Mohammedanism is an uncompromising emphasis upon the absolute transcendence of God, which has as its corollary an insuperable cleavage between God and man which makes God's action upon man purely extrinsic and man's response to God purely one of obedience; the very word *Islam* means 'submission'. Such at least is what may be described as the 'official' interpretation of the Koranic doctrine; but even in the Koran itself there are rare passages which suggest a more intimate relation between the Creator and his creatures, and very early in Islam there appears a movement towards a less frigid and austere conception of religion, which reaches its clearest manifestation in the great Sufi mystics. Thus Dr. Margaret Smith writes as follows:

> Orthodox Islam . . . depicts a God transcendent, incomprehensible, infinitely above and beyond that which he has brought into being, and the Koran emphasises the gulf be-

[1] Massignon, *La Passion d'al Hosayn-ibn-Mansoûr al Hallâj* . . .; Maréchal, *Studies in the Psychology of the Mystics*.

tween the human creature and the Divine Essence, yet man is set apart from the other creatures in being capable of receiving the Divine revelation, and the Koran does give some indication of the possibility of a mystical union.[1]

It was the work of the great eleventh-century theologian al-Ghazali to win a place within the theology of Islam for the fundamental Sufist assertion that a human being can achieve a real union with God, and he did this by insisting that the possibility of such a union does not logically entail a pantheistic doctrine of the world. For it was pantheism—or, if not pantheism in the strict sense, at any rate the doctrine that in the mystical union the mystic's creaturely status is for the time abolished—in which Sufism seemed to its critics to issue. It was as a pantheist that al-Hallaj was condemned and executed at Baghdad in the year 922. 'Hallaj has preached that he was God' was the accusation, and it was alleged that in a moment of ecstasy he had uttered the supreme blasphemy *Ana' al Haqq*, 'I am the Truth'.[2] It is perhaps even more difficult in the case of al-Hallaj than in that of Eckhart and Tauler to know whether the language which is used in the attempt to describe the mystical union is to be taken at its face-value as if it were a carefully formulated

---

[1] Op. cit., p. 144.

[2] Maréchal writes as follows: 'Islam, his accusers objected, demands faith towards God and worship of him; but love for God can be only metaphorical. For real love entails reciprocity; hence a proportion between God and man; hence negation of the divine transcendence' (op. cit., p. 257). This is precisely the objection which, in *Agape and Eros*, the Protestant theologian Nygren brings against Catholic spirituality; cf. Burnaby, *Amor Dei*, p. 15f.

metaphysical assertion; Massignon and Maréchal vigorously defend al-Hallaj from the charge of pantheism or monism of any kind. Certainly plenty of passages can be quoted from him in which God and the speaker are clearly distinguished; he is definitely not a pantheist in the strict sense of one who makes a pure and simple identification of the world with God. It was only in a moment of ecstasy—if at all—that he exclaimed 'I am the Truth!', whereas a Hindu monist might say this in cold blood at any time.[1] The question remains, however, whether the condition which he attained, however transiently, in his supreme mystical experience was interpreted by him as being a momentary loss of creatureliness or as what I have called deified creaturehood.

There is a striking description of the state of union which Dr. Smith quotes from the Sufi gnostic al-Hujwiri:

> If God most glorious manifests his essence to anyone, that one will find all his own essence and attributes and actions utterly absorbed in the light of God's essence and the divine qualities and actions and will; and he sees his essence to be the essence of the one, and his attributes to be the attributes of God, and his actions to be God's actions, because of his complete absorption in union with the Divine; and beyond this stage, there is no further stage of union for man.[2]

It is impossible not to be struck by the similarity between the above passage and this from St. John of the Cross:

[1] I am indebted for this remark to Professor R. C. Zaehner.
[2] Op. cit., p. 217.

All the movements and operations which the soul had afore-
time, and which belonged to the principle and strength of
its natural life, are now in this union changed into divine
movements, dead to their own operation and inclination
and alive in God. . . . So, as has been said, the understanding
of this soul is now the understanding of God; and its will is
the will of God; and its memory is the memory of God; and
its delight is the delight of God; and the substance of this
soul . . . is . . . united in him and absorbed in him, and is thus
God by participation in God.[1]

That language such as this need not imply any loss of
creaturehood is shown by the words, previously quoted,
which I have omitted from the last passage, and which
insist that the substance of the soul 'is not the substance
of God, for into this it cannot be substantially changed'.
It is, however, generally agreed that by the third
century of Islam Sufism had developed a definitely
pantheistic character, and it would certainly be difficult to imagine any orthodox Christian mystic using
language such as this, which Dr. Smith quotes from
al-Bistami:

I have shed my Self as a serpent sheds its skin; then I re-
garded my essence, and I was, myself, He.
    I went from God to God, until they cried from me in me,
saying, 'O thou I!'—i.e., I reached the station of annihila-
tion in God.
    For thirty years God most high was my mirror, now I am
my own mirror, i.e., that which I was I am no more, for
'I' and 'God' represent polytheism, denying his unity. Since

---

[1] *Living Flame*, loc. cit. sup.

I am no more, God most high is his own mirror. Behold, now I say that God is the mirror of myself, for with my tongue he speaks, and I have vanished away.[1]

Paradoxical as it may seem, it is not in fact difficult to understand how Islam, with its doctrine of unqualified divine transcendence, can give rise to this 'pantheistic' mystical doctrine. There is, of course, no place for pantheism in the strict sense, that is, for the view that everything in the world is, from the moment of its first existence, simply identical with God. On the contrary, the difference between God and his creatures will tend to be pushed to the point at which, in contrast to the Christian doctrine that creatures have a dependent reality, it will be held that creatures have no reality at all in virtue of their creation, and that the only reality is God. But when this point is reached, the conclusion will follow that the creature's only hope of achieving reality at all will be by being literally and entitatively changed into its Creator. And since the desire for reality is one of the mainsprings of mystical religion, the desire will create the belief in the possibility of its fulfilment. Having begun with the conviction that we are totally unreal, we end with the conviction that we can become the one supreme and infinite Reality; in this remarkable *enantiodromia* we see another instance of the fact previously noted, that, when the balanced Christian duality is lost, we are left with extreme positions which are essentially unstable and which can swing over with startling suddenness into each other. There is, as I hope

[1] Op. cit., p. 242–3.

to show shortly, a direct connection between the classical Christian doctrine of creatures as dependent realities and the classical Christian doctrine of grace as conferring deified creaturehood. If once we lose our conviction of the reality of creatures in an unbalanced emphasis upon their dependence, we shall be only too likely to compensate for this by a mystical doctrine which transfers us at one swing from a creaturehood which cannot be deified to a deification which destroys creaturehood. I suspect that this may be the fundamental explanation of the way in which Reformation Protestantism, with its unqualified assertion of the sovereignty of God in Calvin and its rejection of all forms of mysticism and pietism in Luther, gave rise to mystics like Jacob Boehme and to the later Lutheran pietist movement. Before we pass on, however, to consider the objections that are brought by Reformation Protestants against the traditional Catholic doctrine of grace and the supernatural, it must be made plain that the foregoing discussion of mysticism is relevant to the Christian life in all its forms.

The reason for this is that, although Christian mysticism is mysticism in its most authentic form, the condition of the Christian mystic is not *essentially* different from that of any Christian who is in a state of grace. It is of course recognized by Catholic theologians that the Christian mystic is the recipient of a most wonderful and transforming gift from God, a gift which, although he can by the ordinary practices of the Christian religion remove the obstacles that might otherwise impede it, he is totally incapable of acquiring by his own efforts, since it is a pure and unpredictable grace of the Creator. But, for the very reason that it is only conferred upon a small minority of good Christians, it cannot be essential to salvation, and no one is more insistent than the Christian mystics themselves that mystical experience is something which one can perfectly well do without and which it is very wrong to go out of one's way to seek. St. John of the Cross expressly directs confessors to tell their penitents 'how much more precious in God's sight is one work or act of the will performed in charity than are all the visions and communications that they may receive from heaven, since these imply neither merit nor demerit'.[1] St. Teresa is characteristically matter-of-fact about those who abandon themselves to spiritual consolations: 'They get it into their heads that it is *arrobamiento*, or rapture. But I call it *abobamiento*, foolishness; for they are doing nothing but wasting their time at it and ruining their health.'[2] The precise ontological nature of mystical experience is a matter of some controversy among the experts; two of the most illuminating discussions of it are provided by Père A. Gardeil's two volumes on *La Structure de l'âme et l'Expérience mystique* and by the second part of M. Jacques Maritain's great work *Distinguer pour unir: les Degrés du Savoir*. It would however be generally agreed that, while the summit of mystical experience is the nearest thing to the beatific vision that any human being can enjoy in this life, it is altogether unnecessary for holiness, since what unites us

[1] *Ascent*, II, xxii, 19; Peers, I, p. 184.
[2] *Interior Castle*, IV, iii; Peers, II, p. 245.

to God is not mystical experience but that supernatural charity which is accessible to the mystic and the non-mystic alike, and furthermore that the condition of the mystic is fundamentally the same as that of the ordinary Christian. Although one can set no limits to the graces that God may see fit to confer upon any particular Christian man or woman (short of an actual entitative conversion of the substance of the soul into the substance of God, or the hypostatic union of his or her human nature to one of the Persons of the Trinity), and although conceivably two degrees of grace successively conferred may differ *quantitatively* (if the term may be allowed) from each other more than the lesser of them differs from the purely natural condition, yet the really decisive *qualitative* change occurs in the primary act of incorporation into Christ, the normal instrument of which is baptism and the necessary development of which is not mystical experience but the life of the supernatural virtues of faith, hope and charity. The point has been very clearly expressed by Mr. E. I. Watkin:

> Since mystical experience is an increase and manifestation of sanctifying grace, it does not differ essentially from the hidden life of grace in the souls of all the just. Throughout the entire process from grace to glory no new principle is introduced. Hence the mystical union-intuition involves no such introduction of a new principle. It is but a development and unfolding of a principle already present. Whereas the infusion of sanctifying grace in our regeneration is a new creation, the mystical way is but the growth of that

new creature, mystical experience a concomitant manifestation of the new life thus growing.[1]

And again:

> The way from sanctifying grace to beatific glory is one continuous road of increasing supernatural union between the soul and God.[2]

There are thus two very striking and fundamental differences between the attitude of Christian and non-Christian spirituality to mysticism. In non-Christian religions mysticism, if it is recognized at all, is looked upon as being the only, or virtually the only, way by which a man may attain beatitude; the mystic's life is altogether unlike that of the ordinary person, and mystical theology is thus totally irrelevant to anyone except mystics. In Catholic Christian spirituality, on the other hand, the life of the mystic is essentially homogeneous with that of any Christian who is in a state of grace; and so, for this very reason, the attempt to describe his experience is directly relevant to the life of the ordinary Christian. For the Christian mystic is simply the Christian to whom the essence of Christian existence has been revealed with peculiar intensity and vividness. When all allowances have been made for the special characteristics of his experience which arise from the peculiar features of his own temperament, his condition of life, his special graces and so on, the fact remains that what he is describing is that life in grace—that state of deified creaturehood—which is the condition of all the baptized. And

---

[1] *Philosophy of Mysticism*, p. 241.
[2] Ibid., p. 129.

the very fact that his stammering attempts to express the ineffable are not wholly incomprehensible to his hearers is the sign that, however obscurely and inchoately, they too have known in its essential nature the experience of which he speaks. What is essential to the Christian life is union with God by faith, hope and charity; it is because the mystic has been given an extraordinary insight into the nature of that union that his utterances are relevant not only to other mystics but to the Church as a whole.

2. THE PROTESTANT PROTEST

We must now turn to consider the objections that are commonly brought by Reformation Protestants (especially those of the present day) against the Catholic doctrine of grace as deification and against the Catholic mystical doctrines in particular. The usual accusation, as we find it for example in Dr. Brunner and Dr. Niebuhr,[1] is that it assumes a 'two-storey' structure of man, which is untrue to the Bible, and also results in an inadequate understanding of the effects of the Fall. The traditional Catholic formulation, which is based upon St. Irenaeus's exegesis of Genesis 1. 26 (though, of course, no one maintains that it necessarily expresses the original meaning of the Hebrew text), distinguishes between the divine image (*eikōn, imago*) in man, which it alleges to be

---

[1] Brunner, *Man in Revolt*, ch. v (c) and App. I; Niebuhr, *The Nature and Destiny of Man*, I, ch. x. Cf. Brunner's note on 'The History of the Doctrine of the *Imago Dei*', in his *Dogmatics*, II, p. 75.

indestructible, and the divine likeness (*homoiōsis, simili-tudo*), which, it asserts, was lost by the Fall, though it can be progressively restored by grace in those who are regenerate. Furthermore, it equates the image with man's natural endowments, sufficient for the living of a good life as a citizen of this world, and the likeness with a *donum superadditum*, which is supernatural both *quoad modum* and *quoad essentiam*, which exceeds anything that man's nature can either demand as of right or obtain by its own efforts, and which is concerned with man's life as a citizen of the other world and with his attainment of the beatific vision. The strictures of Brunner and Neibuhr are the more important because neither of them is extreme in his views of human corruption. Brunner explicitly repudiates the Lutheran teaching that the image of God in man is so completely wrecked that only a 'relic' of it is left, and he even more decisively rejects Barth's view, which apparently denies even the survival of a relic. Niebuhr, again, is prepared to accept the distinction between image and likeness as representing respectively 'man's character as a creature embedded in the natural order' and 'the freedom of his spirit, his transcendance over natural process and finally his self-transcendence', and he considers that 'Protestantism . . . was wrong in asserting that man's essential nature had been destroyed'.[1]

Where, however, both Brunner and Niebuhr disagree with the Catholic doctrine is in their assertion that it introduces into man an unnatural dualism, which sees

[1] Op. cit., I, pp. 286, 292.

man's highest activities as merely an accidental and, as it were, superfluous addition to a nature which could perfectly well find its fulfilment in the things of this world; and that moreover it belittles the effect of sin by affirming that the Fall leaves man's nature essentially unimpaired. Both of them maintain that man's spiritual endowments are rooted in his very nature, and they consider the effect of sin to be neither the loss of the 'likeness', as in Catholic doctrine, nor the destruction of the 'image', as in Lutheran and Barthian doctrine, but rather the perversion and distortion of the image.

I have attempted elsewhere to deal with this objection[1] and I shall not repeat myself more than is necessary here. I think it must be admitted that some of the Catholic manualists have stated the doctrine of grace and nature in a very pedestrian and uninspired way. Certain points need, however, to be remembered. In the first place, the doctrine of nature and supernature in Catholic theology does not mean that the two operate in isolation from each other, like two families living in flats on two different storeys of the same building separated by a soundproof floor. On the contrary, supernature means the supernaturalization of nature, the elevation of nature by grace to a condition that it could not attain by its own powers. Grace requires nature as the raw material in which it works, and its sole *raison d'être* is to do this. Thus St. Thomas Aquinas not only tells us that grace perfects nature without destroying it, but also that grace

[1] *Christ, the Christian and the Church*, p. 222f.

requires nature as its presupposition.[1] Again, when it is
said that man has by nature only a *potentia obedientialis*,
a purely passive càpacity, for receiving grace, it is not
meant that in concrete reality there has ever existed a
'merely natural man'. What it does mean is that God has
in fact elevated man to an order of existence far higher
than is demanded simply by the fact that he is a rational
animal, that, whereas man might have exercised his
reason simply upon the beings around him and upon his
own nature and have been led simply to know God as
the ground of the finite universe, he has in fact been
elevated by God to a participation in God's own life. In
saying that man has by nature a *potentia obedientialis* for
the supernatural order, we are saying that when, rising
in the scale of nature from lifeless matter through vege-
tative and sensitive organisms, we come to the rational
animal man, we have reached a point in which a creature,
while still unable to raise itself above its own level, can
be raised by God to the enjoyment of God himself. In
man's rational character (and the word, of course, covers
far more than 'reason' in the narrow sense, but includes
all those spiritual and cultural powers which distinguish
man from the brute beasts), the natural world has
reached a point at which it can be supernaturalized.
Grace is thus not merely something added to nature, as
an extra storey may be added to a house, but is something that completes and perfects it. Nature is not only

[1] *S. Theol.* I, i, 8 *ad* 2: *Cum enim gratia non tollat naturam sed per-
ficiat* . . . ; ii, 2 *ad* 1: *Sic enim fides praesupponit cognitionem naturalem,
sicut gratia naturam* . . .

accompanied by grace, but is elevated by it. Supernature is neither contrary to nature nor indifferent to it; rather it is nature's fulfilment. The point has been admirably expressed by Père Charlier in the following words:

> What is first in the divine intention and is willed therein defines a being better, from the point of view of the theologian, in its concrete givenness than does its metaphysical constitution. I am first of all a child of God before I am a rational animal . . . There is indeed a radical distinction between the orders of nature and grace. The supernatural order is indeed above the powers and requirements of nature. Furthermore, when we interpret the gifts of grace in philosophical language, we must say that they are accidents, and indeed contingent accidents as regards their relation to nature. But the theologian must not put his stress primarily upon this. . . . Seen in God, our adoptive sonship is the essential element in what God has willed to make of us. Hence, grace does not appear to the theologian as an inherently indifferent *superadditum* to nature. Is it not God's primary design to make us, his creatures, into his children, and to create for this a nature capable of receiving such a gift and altogether directed towards this sublime end?[1]

[1] *Essai sur le Problème théologique*, p. 157. A most illuminating exposition of the way in which the classical doctrine of the supernatural was gradually formulated in Catholic theology has been given by Fr. Henri de Lubac, S.J., in the third part of his book *Surnaturel*. On p. 394 he makes a telling reference to the revolution in the conception of man's nature which has taken place behind an innocent façade when some schools of theology have simply identified the notion of *supernaturale* with that of *superadditum naturae* 'not only in the sense of "a good superadded to a natural good" but of "a finality superadded to a natural finality".'

If such an interpretation as this is accepted, we can say that any impression that the Catholic doctrine of nature and supernature makes an artificial separation between the two orders is at best due to a misunderstanding and at worst only due to the fact that the doctrine has been expressed in the terms of a philosophical system that is inadequate to it. And one would be only too glad to believe that the differences which have separated Catholic and Protestant theologians on the doctrine of grace could be entirely removed by a process of clarification conducted in a friendly atmosphere and that they do not rest upon fundamental theological disagreement. I doubt, however, whether the matter is as simple as this. It is true that the more moderate Protestants, such as Brunner, seem to hold a doctrine of the nature of man as God's creature which approximates to that of Catholicism; he even seems prepared to admit the possibility of natural theology, so long as it is given the name of 'revelation in Creation', though he holds a less hopeful view than most Catholic theologians of the extent to which this revelation has been obscured by sin.[1] In Barth, however, there seems to be a clear denial that man has, in the nature which God has given him, any capacity, however passive, for the reception of grace. Grace, when it is given, appears as something which contradicts and ignores man's natural constitution altogether. For Barth, the fact that 'the possibility of a knowledge corresponding to God's real world has actually been given to man' is 'a *novum* equally inconceivable, and it

[1] Cf. *Dogmatics*, I, p. 135f., 175f.

is contrary to all man's ability and capacity'; 'the possibility of a knowledge of God's Word lies in God's Word and nowhere else'.[1] In statements such as these we are faced with a more violent segregation of grace from nature than anything of which the most plodding Catholic manualist could be guilty, and, as Père Bouyer has shown, it rests upon a further segregation of creation from its Creator:

> The first *cri du coeur* of the Barthian faith, in the Commentary on the Epistle to the Romans, where it is expressed with an intensity and a purity never recovered since, is the formula: *Finitum non capax infiniti*, the finite is not 'capable' of the infinite. Later on Barth discovered that it had too philosophical a sound and substituted for it the formula, more Biblical in its terms, *Homo peccator non capax justitiae Dei*, sinful man is not 'capable' of the justice of God. We may, however, think that the first formula, in its abrupt simplicity and the absolute character of its antithetical contrast, was more faithful to his intuition. The way in which Biblical expressions such as 'Thou art on the earth, and God is in heaven' or 'I will not give my glory to another' recur like leit-motifs under Barth's pen is a perpetual advertisement or reminder of the absoluteness of the divine glory, without any possible limitation whatever, in his living thought. Barth indefatigably reminds us that God is 'the Lord' and that that, in the last resort, is all that his Word wishes to tell us. But it is too little to say that in relation to this incomparable lordship we must admit ourselves to be slaves; we ought rather to

---

[1] O. Weber, *Karl Barth's Church Dogmatics*, p. 30. This Book has been certified by Barth as giving an accurate exposition of his teaching.

say that we are nothing. Not only any comparison, but even any possibility of a real relation between this God and his creature is excluded. Rather than forming such a link, creation—and still more redemption—is the affirmation of its impossibility, of its total absence of significance.[1]

This statement of Bouyer's is all the more impressive because he is far from adopting an attitude of pure hostility to Barth's teaching. 'Here more than ever', he says, 'it is impossible to ignore, in the giddy sprightliness of this glaring nihilism, an apprehension of the sacred greatness of God which has rarely been equalled.'[2]

The point which I wish to make is that there is a direct connection between the extrinsecism of the Protestant doctrine of grace and the nihilism of its doctrine of creation. This may seem to be a sweeping and, indeed, an offensive assertion, and I wish to indicate its precise scope. I do not wish to suggest that the fundamental insights of the Reformers were mistaken; as Bouyer has shown, the doctrines that salvation is a free gift from God (*sola gratia*), that God's sovereignty is absolute (*soli Deo gloria*), that we are justified through faith, that the Scriptures are the Word of God—all these are part of the traditional Catholic scheme, however much the popular religion and the ecclesiastical politics of the later Middle Ages and the Renaissance may have forgotten them. And in the writings of Luther and Calvin themselves, to say nothing of the lives of many saintly Lutherans and Calvinists, there are clear indications that

[1] *Du Protestantisme à l'Église*, p. 92, reproduced by permission of the Harvill Press Ltd.   [2] Ibid., p. 93.

grace does not merely impute to man a righteousness
that he can never acquire but also transforms and super-
naturalizes his whole being. What then, Bouyer enquires
is the source of the radical extrinsecism which charac-
terizes the official Protestant theology, which makes of
grace, in Luther's words, nothing but a cloak cast over
a corpse? It is due, he replies, to the uncritical adoption
of some of the worst features of decadent late medieval
scholasticism.

> Their own construction of their own principles is inaccept-
> able only because they made it out of the uncriticised
> materials of that decomposing Catholicism from which
> they wished to escape but to which they remained captive
> to an extent which they seem never to have suspected.
> There are few phrases that so clearly reveal the hidden sick-
> ness of the Reformation which was going to rot all its fruits
> as the words in which Luther says that the only scholastic
> in whom there was any good was Ockham. . . .
>   And what indeed was the essential characteristic of the
> thought of Ockham and of nominalism in general but a
> radical empiricism which reduces a being to its perceptible
> aspects, which empties away with the very notion of sub-
> stance not only all possibility of real relations between be-
> ings but also all stability and consistency in any of them,
> and finally withdraws all intelligibility from the real and
> conceives God himself only as an inapprehensible proteus?
>   Under these conditions a grace which changes something
> in us while remaining a pure grace of God becomes unthink-
> able. Otherwise something is genuinely changed in us, and
> then this change comes from us, and to suppose that it could
> in addition come from God beforehand would be equivalent

to confusing God with his creature. No way can be seen of avoiding these consequences once we have admitted that I am my experience and my experience is myself. If being is reduced to action, and action to our experience of it, then either our experience is closed to everything that is transcendent, or else, if in spite of this the transcendent could intervene, it could do it only by degrading itself and reducing itself to a part of ourselves.

Thus it will follow, no less radically, that grace, in order to remain grace, in order to remain a pure gift of God, will have to remain entirely external to us, but also, on the other hand, that faith, in order to remain our own, in order to avoid falling into an extrinsecism which would empty out of a man all the reality of his religion, will have to remain as it were shut up in ourselves.[1]

Thus, for Bouyer, the negative and 'heretical' aspect of the Reformation arises precisely from its failure to be sufficiently radical, from the survival in Protestantism of the 'most irremediably vitiated and corrupt' elements of late medieval thought.[2] He adds that the anti-protestant Catholic controversialists were no less entangled in these snares than the Protestants themselves, and that in consequence they were unable to refute Protestants without at the same time repudiating the truths which the Protestants had grasped.

Never for a moment do we escape from the alternatives. Either a grace which alone saves us, but saves us without touching us, or else a grace which saves us by our independent co-operation, so that strictly speaking we have to

---

[1] Op. cit., p. 164f.   [2] Ibid., p. 176.

save ourselves. Either a faith which is faith in our own faith, that is in our immediate experience and ultimately in that alone, or else a faith which is a pure and simple abdication of ourselves. Either a God who is everything, so that man and the world are literally nothing, or else a world and man which have limited but real powers and values, and then a God who is only the first in a series, a magnified creature but not the creator. Either a Word which remains absolutely foreign to us, which man can only falsify but never interpret and which has no possible meaning for him, or else a word which in the last resort is only his own, in which he himself gives both questions and answers and presumes to attribute to God what is only his own invention.[1]

The same phenomenon, Bouyer remarks, is to be observed in the realms of spirituality. He comments on

the constant and surprising similarities between the spiritual doctrines elaborated in the Protestant Reformation and in Counter-Reformation Catholicism. There is the same psychologism on both sides, the same voluntarism, the same activism, the same constant appeal to personal decision, to interior 'conversion' and lastly to an incessant militant activity. A striking example of this agreement between separated brethren, which not only existed but became more emphatic to the precise degree in which the separation became sharper, is provided by the work of Angelus Silesius. Those of his verses which have seemed to hasty critics to be most characteristic of his passage to Catholicism and his adherence to the Counter-Reformation are often those in which he merely puts Lutheran sentences into verse![2]

This comment seems to me to be both true and illu-

[1] Ibid., p. 166.   [2] Ibid., p. 122.

minating, and the doctrine of grace is not the only branch of theology in which Protestants and Catholics alike have taken over uncritically and unconsciously some of the least desirable features of late medieval thought; I have shown elsewhere at some length how this happened in the theology of the Eucharist.[1] It would, of course, be absurd to maintain—nor does Bouyer suggest it—that something as catastrophic in its consequence as the nihilistic strand in Protestantism was due simply to the fact that the Reformers had read the wrong kind of philosophy; it has causes which lie far deeper, on the psychological and religious levels. Nevertheless, there is profound significance in the fact that Luther found Ockham's nominalism so attractive, and it emphasizes the close relation that there is between doctrines of nature and of supernature. For if man was what Ockham thought he was, grace could hardly do anything but what Luther thought it did. If the whole being of a creature consists in its perceptible qualities, then grace may involve a changed attitude to the creature on the part of God and a new manner of behaviour on the part of man, but it cannot involve a supernaturalization of man's inner substance beneath the perceptible level, for man has no inner substance to be supernaturalized. As we have seen, it was not only Protestantism that was infected with nominalism; there were chairs of nominalist theology in the universities of sixteenth-century Spain.[2] What is, however, striking is

[1] *Corpus Christi*, ch. iv, v.
[2] I am indebted for information on this point to Fr. Copleston, S.J.

how very much more successful Catholic theology has
been than Protestant theology in recent years in shaking
off this encumbrance and recovering the authentic tradition. It is possible that, in some details, Père Bouyer has
overstated his case, but that case is, I think, fundamentally sound. It has been endorsed by Professor H. A.
Hodges in a quite independent discussion of redemption,
justification and grace. 'It has long seemed to me,' he
writes, 'and I think history confirms it, that the Reformation principle of the sovereign grace of God is set forth
and embodied in Catholic teaching and practice not less
truly, and a good deal less abstractly, than in the Reformation doctrines themselves.'[1]

3. GRACE, CREATION AND DEIFICATION

How, then, shall we define grace? Grace is, I shall say,
a participation in the life of God himself, which, in a
human being, is normally, but not invariably, brought
about by incorporation into the human nature of Christ.
(It will be clear that we are at the moment concerned
with what theologians call 'sanctifying grace' or *gratia
gratum faciens*, which is a condition or *habitus* of the
human subject, and not with 'actual grace' or *gratia gratis
data*, which is supernatural assistance for the perform-
ance of acts by which others as well as the subject himself are to be made pleasing to God.)

To be a child of God . . . [writes Père Mersch] is an ontological reality, so great as to be of a different order from

[1] *The Pattern of Atonement*, p. 101.

every created magnitude, to overflow our intellectual categories, to be truly mysterious, and to be capable of definition as regards what it is in itself only in terms of that which defines God as he is in himself.[1]

And again:

The infinite Being has two ways of giving himself to finite beings; by the former, he gives himself to them in *their* way, which makes them themselves; by the latter he gives himself to them in *his* way, which makes them one with him.[2]

To be in a state of grace, then, means not just to be living with our own life, though that itself is a pure gift from God and is sustained only by his incessant creative and conserving activity, but to be living with God's life. This is a notion which is exceedingly difficult from the point of view of the unenlightened human intellect. Like all theological notions it must be understood analogically, and there is nothing precisely like it except itself. That a creature, radically and inconvertibly distinct and diverse from its Creator, should yet be elevated to an order of being and activity in which, remaining the finite subject which it is, it has as the principle of its life and energy not only itself but God; that a finite being can be the subject of an activity that is not finite but divine—this might well seem to be both inconceivable and impossible, were it not that quite ordinary Christians enjoy an experience which it is impossible ade-

[1] 'Filii in Filio', in *Nouvelle Revue Théologique*, July 1938, p. 825.
[2] Ibid., p. 820.

quately to describe in any other way. The intellectual difficulty involved appears clearly when St. Thomas Aquinas attempts to describe grace and its workings by applying the categories of the Aristotelian psychology. Grace, he tells us, 'implies something in the soul', *ponit aliquid in anima;*[1] it is not a virtue, for virtues are perfections of the powers of the soul, whereas grace is the source of the supernatural virtues and so must lie deeper than the virtues, in the very essence of the soul.[2] Grace is, in fact, a *quality of the soul.* God

> so provides for natural creatures that he does not only move them to natural acts, but also bestows upon them certain forms and powers which are the principles of their acts, so that they may of themselves be inclined to such acts . . . Much more, then, into those which he moves to follow the eternal supernatural good does he infuse certain supernatural forms or qualities, whereby they may be moved by him gently and promptly to seek the eternal good. And so the gift of grace is a certain quality.[3]

It would obviously be easy to interpret St. Thomas as meaning simply that grace is a disposition which God brings about in the depths of the soul as a result of which we tend more readily and promptly to seek our supernatural beatitude, in much the same sort of way in which our natural dispositions enable us to seek more efficiently our earthly well-being. And, although the Angelic Doctor indeed describes the light of grace, in the phrase of the Second Petrine Epistle, as 'the partici-

[1] *S. Theol.*, II, I, cx, I.   [2] Ibid., 3, 4.   [3] Ibid., 2c.

pation of the divine nature',[1] we might also recall that
he employs the term 'participation' to describe the relation of dependence and likeness which all things have to
God simply by their creation.[2] It is thus perhaps not
altogether surprising that some theologians of the
Eastern Orthodox Church have rejected altogether the
Western doctrine of the 'created supernatural' as postu-
lating a far too extrinsic and insufficiently intimate union
between God and his children.[3] I shall return to this
point shortly. At the moment I wish to suggest that this
appearance of extrinsecism in St. Thomas is due mainly
to the difficulty of giving a rational account of grace in
the highly naturalistic system of Aristotelian psychology.
There is, of course, a penumbra of indefiniteness about
such words as 'participation' and 'likeness' which makes
their precise meaning in any context sometimes difficult
to determine, but it is at least significant that, when he
is talking of the theology rather than the psychology of
grace, St. Thomas can write a passage like the following,
which occurs in his argument 'that God alone is the
cause of grace':

> The gift of grace exceeds every faculty of a created nature;
> since it is nothing else than a certain participation of the
> divine nature, which exceeds every other nature. And so it
> is impossible that any creature should cause grace. For it is

---

[1] Ibid., 3c: *Hoc autem est in ordine ad naturam divinam participatam....
Ipsum lumen gratiae, quod est participatio divinae naturae ...*

[2] Ibid., I, xliv, 1c: *Relinquitur ergo quod omnia alia a Deo non sint
suum esse, sed participant esse ... diversificantur secundum diversam partici-
pationem essendi.*

[3] Cf. V. Lossky, *Théologie Mystique de l'Église d'Orient*, p. 85.

as necessary that God alone should deify, by bestowing a
share (*consortium*) of the divine nature by a certain participation of likeness, as it is impossible that anything except fire
should kindle.[1]

It is therefore not surprising that the Angelic Doctor
goes on to say that one thing on the level of grace is
greater than the whole universe on the level of nature.[2]

I am not, however, particularly concerned to defend
St. Thomas from criticism. I have referred to him mainly
in order to illustrate the extreme difficulty of this conception of grace as deifying, without destroying, the
creature. The one contribution which I should wish to
make to the discussion is to suggest that the whole possibility of man's deification depends upon two facts. The
first is the fact that God is incessantly active as Creator
at the ontological root of every creature, maintaining it
in existence by, as it were, continually pouring his goodness into it. The second is the fact that man, as a rational
and responsible being, is made, as no lower creature is,
in the image of God. If we hold a deistic view of
creation—and I fear that many Christians allow themselves to think as deists when they are off their guard—
we shall think of creatures as incapsulated in their finitude in such a way as to make them incapable of receiving anything more than purely external manipulation by
God. He can push them about, but he cannot bring
about any inner transformation in them; at least he can-

---

[1] *S. Theol.*, II, I, cxii, 1c.
[2] *Bonum gratiae unius majus est quam bonum naturae totius universi*
(ibid., cxiii, 9 *ad* 2).

not do this without destroying their natures and making them into other beings than they are. For the deist, as for the ancient Greek, every being has a nicely rounded off nature, which contains from the start, at any rate implicitly, all that it can ever become; all that it can ever be arises simply from the unfolding of its primary constitution. The very notion of the supernatural is a contradiction; the nature of a thing is *to ti ēn einai*, 'what it was meant to be', and to suppose that it was meant to be anything more would be nonsense. Even to say that a being is finite is to say that it is *finitum*, finished, rounded off, complete.

In contrast with this view, the Christian doctrine of finite beings as dependent realities means that it is the essence of the finite to be *incomplete*. The very bounds which circumscribe it witness to the region that lies beyond it for its exploration. And so far from being sealed off, it depends upon God for that incessant activation without which it would cease to be. It is true, as we have already seen, that we ought not to interpret this in a pejorative sense. Although it is true that, if God ceased conserve a creature, it would cease to exist, the fundamental truth is that so long as God conserves it it goes on existing, and exists with all those energies and perfections which he communicates to it. Nevertheless, the mere fact that it is not self-existent means that it is not ontologically incapsulated in itself; to be a finite being is to be essentially *open*, open to the activity of God, who, without annulling or withdrawing anything that he has given, can always give more. Thus, the *potentia obedien-*

tialis of nature for grace is not a kind of afterthought or accident; it arises out of the very notion of a finite creature as Christian theology sees it. But the *kind* of *potentia obedientialis*—the type of perfectibility of which it is capable without its nature being suppressed— will, of course, depend upon the kind of creature that it is, and it is here that our second point comes in, that man is made in the image of God. To put the matter briefly, to be in God's image is to be capable of possessing God's life. The coeternal Son, who is the Father's coequal Image, possesses the life of God in his own right. In contrast, a finite being made in God's image is capable of possessing that life only if God raises him to it. Barth was, I believe, profoundly wrong when he wrote the words *Finitum non capax infiniti*; and, by one of those *enantiodromiae* which we have so often had occasion to notice, he had unwittingly slipped into a typically Greek attitude to finite existence. The truth, I suggest, is the precise opposite. *Finitum capax infiniti*; to be finite is to be incessantly dependent upon God and receiving existence from him; it is therefore to be inherently *open to God*. *Finitum capax infiniti* does not mean that a man can raise himself to the possession of God by his own powers, but it does mean that he can be rasied to it by God, and that, if he is so raised, all his natural powers will thereby be enriched and ennobled.

No one, I think, could deny that this unconfused interpenetration of the finite by the Infinite, of the creature by the Creator, of dependent by self-existent being, is both surprising and mysterious. I do not think, however, that it presents insuperable difficulties for our minds once we recognize that the creative act of God, while it posits the creature in existence as an utterly dependent being, radically different in its ontological status from the self-existent Being who gives it everything that it has, establishes it, by that very fact, as not separated from God but most intimately related to him. Here more than elsewhere we must refuse to be deceived by the misleading notion of a 'gulf' between God and the creature. If there were a gulf, then the creature would be cut off by it from the source of its being and would collapse into non-existence. It is because there is no gulf, but on the contrary a never failing inflow of creative power, that there is a world at all. It is indeed true that the divine activity which deifies a creature by grace is of an immensely higher order than the divine activity which creates and conserves it; we can describe this, as we cannot describe creation, as an *interpenetration* of the created by the divine. Interpenetration, however, does not mean confusion; there is no blurring of the distinction between self-existent and dependent being. The very possibility of deification by grace arises from the fact that creation is a most intimate and incessant donation of the creature to itself by God; it is not a projection of the creature into a lonely and isolated vacuum.

The most mysterious and profound example of this interpenetration of the finite by the infinite which we call grace is, of course, provided by the assumption of human nature by the divine Word in the Incarnation; as we saw in the last chapter, it was only by the most

strenuous efforts that the Church was able to maintain
her faith in an unconfused union of the two natures,
against those who would have made things easier for the
intellect to grasp either by converting the finite nature
into the infinite, like the Eutychians, or by separating
the two natures from each other, like the Nestorians.
We ought not to let familiarity blind us to the astound-
ing nature of the claim which the orthodox doctrine
makes, that the infinite and self-existent God can be, and
is the subject of a finite nature and a finite mode of
existence. The union of two natures, a human and a
divine, in one person infinitely exceeds in its wonder
and its mystery the union of many persons in the human
nature of Christ, which is what we normally have in
mind when we speak of grace. None the less, for all its
uniqueness, the Incarnation is an example—and indeed
the supreme culmination—of the notion of deified
creaturehood; and this is why theologians are accustomed, when discussing the Incarnation, to speak of
gratia unionis, 'the grace of union'.[1] The assumption of
manhood into God, of which the Athanasian Creed
speaks, is so far reaching that, while the human and the
divine are distinct as *natures*, the human has no distinct
existence as *person*, but is constituted in the divine Person
of the pre-existent Word; this is why, in our worship
of Christ, we do not have to discriminate between an
uncreated part which is adorable and a created part
which it would be idolatry to adore, but are able to pay
one undivided act of adoration to the one Christ, since

[1] Cf. *S. Theol.*, III, ii, 10–12.

all homage, to whichever nature it is directed, passes through the nature to the Person in which the nature is constituted and consists. In contrast we may recall that, although the saints are partakers of the divine nature by sanctifying grace, we cannot adore them without falling into idolatry; and the reason for this is that, although they have by grace a common participation in the divine nature, the saints retain their individual finite created persons and so can rightly be given only a creaturely homage. Nevertheless, both in the union of the two natures in one Person in the Incarnation, and in the union of many persons with the divine nature by grace, we are concerned with a deification of the creaturely, and so, with all due precautions, we can speak in each case of the activity of grace.

4. DIVINE ENERGY, OR THE CREATED SUPERNATURAL?

I referred a little way back to the misgivings which some Eastern Orthodox theologians feel about what they consider to be the materialistic and extrinsicist Western doctrine of the 'created supernatural' or 'created grace', and I shall devote the remainder of this chapter to a consideration of them. It may clear the air to point out at the start that both parties to the discussion are determined to maintain the distinctness of the two terms involved and also the reality of their union. Both are agreed that we are concerned with the *deification of man*; neither is setting up as a champion of Protestantism. Man remains man, nevertheless he is deified; those are the agreed terms of the problem; the question is simply whether the classical Western formulation of the situation does it justice.

The difference between the Eastern and the Western outlook begins very far back in connection with the doctrine of creation and indeed of God himself. I have discussed it fairly thoroughly in my book *Existence and Analogy*,[1] and I shall give only a brief summary here. For Western theology, God is fundamentally knowable; he knows himself perfectly, and his very understanding is his essence.[2] Theologians such as Nicholas of Cusa, with his God who is a fundamentally incomprehensible *coincidentia oppositorum*, have been something of an oddity in the West. In Eastern Christendom, however, where the writings of the pseudo-Areopagite have received rather less reinterpretation than in the West, the notion of God as, in his essence, incomprehensible has taken very deep root. This tendency, insists M. Vladimir Lossky, in his important study *La Théologie Mystique de l'Église d'Orient*, is not to be written off as neo-Platonism:

> The God of Dionysius, unknowable by nature, the God of the Psalms 'who makes the shadows his hiding-place', is not the primordial unity which is the God of the neo-Platonists. If he is unknowable, it is not in virtue of a simplicity which would be unable to accommodate itself to the multiplicity infecting all our knowledge relative to beings; it is, so to speak, a more fundamental, an absolute

[1] Op. cit., p. 148f.
[2] Cf. S. Theol., I, xiv, 2, 3, 4. *Ex necessitate sequitur quod ipsum ejus intelligree sit ejus essentia et ejus esse* (4c).

unknowability. In fact, if it had for its basis the simplicity
of the One, as in Plotinus, God would not be unknowable
by nature. But in Dionysius it is precisely unknowability
that is the only proper definition of God, if indeed we can
speak in this connection of proper definitions at all.[1]

God is, then, in his essence entirely unknowable and incommunicable. Yet we know that he manifests and
communicates himself in creation, and if we are Christians we believe that he reveals and communicates
himself in an even higher way. To account for this, re-
course is had to a discrimination which is made in the
Areopagitica between the 'unions' (*henōseis*) and the 'distinctions' (*diakriseis*) in God. The unions are altogether
interior to the superessential nature of God and cannot
be externally manifested, while the distinctions are 'processions' (*proodoi*), 'manifestations' (*ekphanseis*) or
'powers' (*dynameis*), in which everything that exists
participates, making God known through creatures.
This doctrine received its definitive statement from the
fourteenth-century Archbishop of Thessalonica, St.
Gregory Palamas, by whom an explicit contrast was
made between the 'essence' (*ousia*) of God and his 'energies' (*energeiai*). Two cautions are given. First, 'an
energy is not a divine function in relation to creatures,
although God creates and operates by his energies,
which penetrate everything that exists. Creatures might
not exist, but God would still manifest himself outside
his essence, as the sun shines in its beams beyond the
solar disc, whether or not there are beings capable of

[1] Op. cit., p. 29.

receiving its light.' Secondly, 'the created world does not become infinite and coeternal with God from the fact that the natural processions or the divine energies are such. The energies imply no necessity of creation, which is a free act, effectuated by the divine energy but determined by a decision of the common divine will of the three Persons.'[1]

The full bearing of this doctrine is seen when we consider not God's action in creation but his operation in the order of grace, in our elevation into the life of God himself. I shall quote M. Lossky at length:

> In what respect can we enter into union with the Holy Trinity? If we could at a given moment find ourselves united with the very essence of God, and share it in any degree whatever, we should not be at that moment what we now are, we should be God by nature. God would not then be Trinity but *myrihypostatos*, a God with thousands of hypostases, for he would have as many hypostases as persons sharing in his essence. So, then, God remains inaccessible to us as regards his essence. Can we say, then, that we enter into union with one of the three divine Persons? But this would be the hypostatic union which is proper uniquely to the Son, to the God who becomes man without ceasing to be the Second Person of the Trinity. While we share the same human nature, while we receive in Christ the name of sons of God, we do not become, by the fact of the Incarnation, the divine hypostasis of the Son. We can, then, share neither in the essence nor in the Persons of the Trinity. Nevertheless, the divine promise cannot be an illusion: we are called to share in the divine nature. We must then admit

[1] Ibid., p. 72.

an ineffable distinction in God which is other than that of the essence and the Persons, a distinction as a result of which God will be at the same time accessible and totally inaccessible in different respects. This is the distinction between God's essence or nature in the strict sense, which is inaccessible, unknowable and incommunicable, and his divine energies or operations, natural forces inseparable from the essence, in which God proceeds outwards and manifests, communicates and gives himself. 'The divine and deifying illumination and grace is not the essence but the energy of God', a 'common force and operation of the Trinity'. Thus, as St. Gregory Palamas says, 'in saying that the divine nature is participable not in itself but in its energies, we remain within the limits of piety'.[1]

It is clear that the problem with which the Athonite father is grappling is the same as that which exercised the Western scholastics: how can we give a rational account of the fact that a human being, while remaining a creature, can nevertheless really share in the life of God; and they are equally insistent that there can be neither, on the one hand, a degradation of God nor, on the other, a destruction of the creature's creaturehood. The metaphysical and theological systems which are pressed into service are, however, strikingly different. The Palamite doctrine, for example, ignores altogether the sharp distinction between the orders of nature and supernature which has become classical in the West. For Western theology, in the words of Mersch which have been already quoted, 'the infinite Being has two ways of giving himself to finite beings; by the former, he gives himself

[1] Ibid., p. 67f.

to them in *their* way and makes them themselves; by the latter, he gives himself to them in *his* way which makes them one with him'. But in the Palamite theory, God gives himself in only one way, whether in nature or in grace (if indeed the Palamite would admit this distinction at all); he gives himself in his energies. For the Thomist, grace means a communication of the Creator to the creature in the created mode under which alone a creature can receive anything; for the Palamite, it means a communication of the uncreated energy of God, though not of his incommunicable essence. I have summarized the kind of theological repartee which this situation can produce in the following conversation, which is based upon an actual discussion.

The Palamite opens against the Thomist: 'You make no distinction between the essence of God and his energy and you say that God gives himself to the creature in a finite mode. On your showing, this must mean that the divine essence is given in a finite mode, and this is plainly impossible. Either what is given is finite, in which case it cannot be God, or what is given is God, in which case it cannot be given finitely. In the former case there is no real deification of man; in the latter case man ceases to be a creature. Neither alternative is admissible, so your theory must be false.' The Thomist replies: 'The whole matter is, of course, a profound mystery, but you have not been fair to my thought. I did not mean that God-in-a-finite-mode was given to the creature, but that God was received by the creature in a finite mode. The finitude is in the mode of participation, not in the object participated. And here is a dilemma for you, in return for that on which you tried to impale me. You say that the creature participates in the divine energy, though not in the divine essence. Now listen. Either the energy and the essence are identical, or else in participating in the energy the creature does not really participate in God. In the former case your own theory is false, in the latter it fails to provide for a real deification of man.' 'No,' the Palamite rejoins, 'now it is you who are being unfair to me. The energy is divine, and therefore in participating in the divine energy the creature participates in God. God is present, really present, in his energy as much as in his essence. The only difference is that the energy is communicable and the essence is not. Thus God is really communicated in his energy, though he remains incommunicable in his essence.' 'Really', protests the Thomist, 'this is intolerable. God and his essence cannot be separated. If the energy communicates God it communicates his essence. And then you need my theory to explain how the creature can participate in God without losing its creatureliness.' And so the debate goes on, and there seems little prospect of its ceasing.[1]

I am bound to say that, as a doctrine of the relation between God and his creatures, the Palamite doctrine seems to me to be profoundly unsatisfactory. The notion that God is in his essence fundamentally unintelligible seems to me to be false, and the distinction between the essence and the energies of God is one of which I find it

[1] The above passage is adapted from pp. 151f. of my book *Existence and Analogy*.

almost impossible to make sense. But it does not seem to
me to be in the least heretical, and it preserves the essential Christian attitudes to God and the world. It sees the
created order as a dependent reality, in the sense in
which that notion was expounded in the first chapter of
this book, and it provides for a genuine deification of
man while at the same time preserving man's creaturely
status. While refusing to make the distinction between
nature and supernature in the traditional Western way,
it maintains that fundamental openness of the creature to
unlimited influxes of divine generosity which it is the
primary concern of the distinction between nature and
supernature to provide. We need not therefore be surprised to find an Eastern Orthodox writer saying:

> It cannot be too often repeated: there is no chasm between
> Eastern and Western Christianity. The fundamental prin-
> ciples of Christian spirituality are the same in the East and
> in the West; the methods are very often alike; the differ-
> ences do not bear on the main points. On the whole, there
> is *one* Christian spirituality with, here and there, some
> variations of stress and emphasis.[1]

Neither the Thomist nor the Palamite theory has exhaust-
ed the mystery with which it is preoccupied, nor should
we expect it to do so. The communication of the Creator
to the creature or, to state the matter from the other end,
the elevation of the creature into the life of the Creator
is a mystery so profound, so wonderful, and so far beyond anything which we could have suspected that we
need not be surprised if our various attempts to describe

[1] *Orthodox Spirituality*, by a Monk of the Eastern Church, p. viii.

it run into apparent conflict with one another. I suggested earlier in this chapter that there is a close connection between grace as the deification of creaturehood and creaturehood as dependent reality. And indeed, if we look back at the course which the argument of this book has followed, we shall, I think, see that we have not been concerned simply with the application of a principle of theological method to four independent and unconnected problems, but that the four problems are themselves interrelated and that the discussion of any one of them throws light upon the others. We have seen in the present chapter that our fourth duality, that of deified creaturehood, depends for the very possibility of its actualization upon the first, namely that of dependent reality, and the link between them is provided by the second and the third, which together speak of the assumption of human nature by the Father's coequal and coeternal Son.

> The Incarnation [writes the Angelic Doctor] holds up to man an ideal of that blessed union whereby the created intellect is joined, in an act of understanding, to the uncreated Spirit. It is no longer incredible that a creature's intellect should be capable of union with God by beholding the divine essence, since the time when God became united to man by taking a human nature to himself.
>
> Lastly, the Incarnation puts the finishing touch to the whole vast work envisaged by God. For man, who was the last to be created, returns by a sort of circulatory movement to his first beginning, being united by the work of the Incarnation to the very principle of all things.[1]

[1] *Comp. Theol.*, I, cci.

BIBLIOGRAPHY

BENEDICTINE OF STANBROOK, A, *Mediaeval Mystical Tradition and St. John of the Cross*. London: Burns, Oates. 1954.

BINDLEY, T. H., *The Oecumenical Documents of the Faith*. London: Methuen. 2nd ed., 1950.

BRUNNER, E., *Dogmatics. Vol. I: The Christian Doctrine of God*. London: Lutterworth Press. 1949.

——*Dogmatics. Vol. II: The Christian Doctrine of Creation and Redemption*. London: Lutterworth Press. 1952.

——*Man in Revolt: A Christian Anthropology*. London: Lutterworth Press. 1939.

BRUNNER, E. AND BARTH, K., *Natural Theology*. London: Bles. 1946.

BOUYER, L., *Du Protestantisme et l'Église*. Paris: Éd. du Cerf. 1954.

BURNABY, J. *Amor Dei: A Study of the Religion of St. Augustine*. London: Hodder and Stoughton. 1938.

CHARLIER, L. *Essai sur le Problème Théologique*. Thuillies: Ramgal. 1938.

COPLESTON, F., *A History of Philosophy*. London: Burns, Oates. Vol. II, 1950.

DE LUBAC, H., *Surnaturel*. Paris: Aubier. 1946.

FARRER, A. M., *Finite and Infinite*. London: Dacre Press. 1943.

——*The Glass of Vision*, London: Dacre Press. 1948.

FISCHER, K., *Descartes and his School*. London: Unwin. 1890.

GALTIER, P., *L'Unité du Christ*. Paris: Beauchesne. 1939.

GARDEIL, A., *La Structure de l'Ame et l'Expérience Mystique*. Paris: Gabalda. 2 vols., 1927.

GILSON, É., *La Philosophie au Moyen Age*. Paris: Payot. 2nd ed., 1944.

HODGES, H. A., *The Pattern of Atonement*. London: S.C.M. 1955.

HODGSON, L., *The Doctrine of the Trinity*. London: Nisbet. 1943.

JALLAND, T. G., *The Life and Times of St. Leo the Great*. London: S.P.C.K. 1941.

JOHN OF THE CROSS, ST., *The Complete Works of St. John of the Cross*. Translated by E. Allison Peers. London: Burns, Oates. 3 vols., 1943.

LEWIS, C. S., *Miracles*. London: Bles. 1947.

LOSSKY, V., *La Théologie Mystique de l'Église d'Orient*. Paris: Aubier. 1944.

MARÉCHAL, J., *Studies in the Psychology of the Mystics*. London: Burns, Oates. 1927.

MARITAIN, J., *Distinguer pour unir: Les Degrés du Savoir*. Paris: Desclée de Brouwer. 2nd ed., 1932.

MASCALL, E. L., *Christ, the Christian and the Church*. London: Longmans. 2nd ed., 1955.

——*Corpus Christi*. London: Longmans. 1953.

——*Existence and Analogy*. London: Longmans. 1949.

——*He Who Is: a Study in Traditional Theism*. London: Longmans. 2nd ed., 1948.

MASCARENHAS, H. O., *The Quintessence of Hinduism*. Bombay: St. Sebastian Goan High School. 1951.

MASSIGNON, L., *La Passion d'al Hosayn-ibn-Mansoûr al Hallâj, Martyre mystique d'Islam*. Paris: Geuthner. 2 vols., 1922.

MONK OF THE EASTERN CHURCH, A, *Orthodox Spirituality*. London: S.P.C.K. 1945.

168   *Bibliography*

NIEBUHR, R., *The Nature and Destiny of Man.* London: Nisbet. Vol. I, 1941.

NYGREN, A., *Agape and Eros.* London: S.P.C.K. 2nd ed., 1953.

PHILLIPS, G. E., *The Religions of the World.* Wallington: Religious Education Press. 1948.

PHILLIPS, R. P., *Modern Thomistic Philosophy.* London: Burns, Oates. Vol. II, 1935.

PONTIFEX, M., *The Existence of God.* London: Longmans. 1947.

PONTIFEX, M., AND TRETHOWAN, I., *The Meaning of Existence.* London: Longmans. 1953.

PRESTIGE, G. L., *Fathers and Heretics.* London: S.P.C.K. 1940.

——*God in Patristic Thought.* London: S.P.C.K. 2nd ed., 1952.

QUICK, O. C., *Doctrines of the Creed.* London: Nisbet. 1938.

RAVEN, C. E., *Apollinarianism.* Cambridge Univ. Press. 1923.

RELTON, H. M., *A Study in Christology.* London: S.P.C.K. 1917.

RUYSBROECK, J. VAN, *The Spiritual Espousals.* Translated by E. Colledge. London: Faber. 1952.

SELLERS, R. V., *The Council of Chalcedon.* London: S.P.C.K. 1953.

SERTILLANGES, A. D., *L'Idée de Création.* Paris: Aubier. 1945.

SMITH, M., *Studies in Early Mysticism in the Near and Middle East.* London: Sheldon Press. 1931.

TEMPLE, W., *Christus Veritas.* London: Macmillan. 1924.

——*Nature, Man and God.* London: Macmillan. 1934.

WATKIN, E. I., *The Philosophy of Mysticism.* London: Grant Richards. 1920.

WIGRAM, W. A., *The Separation of the Monophysites.* London: Faith Press. 1923.

WEBER, O., *Karl Barth's Church Dogmatics.* London: Lutterworth Press. 1953.

INDEX

Acacius of Melitene, 97
Aetius of Constantinople, 97
Algazel, 19, 128
Anastasius, 85
Angelus Silesius, 146
Anselm, St., 53
Apollinarius, 81f., 87, 101
Arius, 31, 53f., 82
Athanasius, St., 54, 59f., 69, 80f.,
    87, 98, 122
Augustine of Hippo, St., 42, 53,
    70f., 110f., 122
Averroes, 19
Avicenna, 17f.

Barth, K., 35f., 137f., 154
Basil, St., 60f., 81
Beethoven, L. van, 5, 6
Benedict of Aniane, St., 52
Bergson, H., 34
Berkeley, G., 4, 10, 11
Bindley, T. H., 97
Bistami, al-, 130
Bloemardinne, 124
Boehme, J., 132
Bonaventure, St., 30
Bouyer, L., 142f.
Brunner, E., 35f., 136f.

Burnaby, J., 128

Calvin, J., 10, 70, 132, 143
Cauchy, A. L., 6
Charlier, L., 140
Chekhov, A. P., 11
Colledge, E., 125
Constantine, 57
Coomaraswamy, A., 27
Copleston, F., 18, 147
Cyril of Alexandria, St., 69, 85f.,
    100, 104
de Lubac, H., 140
de Vere, A., 120
Descartes, R., 9
Dionysius of Alexandria, 52
Dionysius of Rome, 52
Dionysius the Pseudo-Areopag-
    ite, 101, 158
Duns Scotus, 19

Eckhart, J., 124, 128
Eutyches, 87f.

Farrer, A. M., 30, 36, 39
Fischer, K., 9
Flavian of Constantinople, 91f.
Francis of Assisi, St., 46